In spite of our best efforts to stay on track, we sometimes find ourselves reverting to old ways of thinking, feeling, and behaving, even when we know better.

Relapse can sneak up on us, linger, and become as confusing as our original codependency. Or it can be brief. Sometimes, we're reacting to other people's craziness. Sometimes, we're reacting to ourselves. Sometimes, we're reacting to the years of training we've had in how to be codependent. Sometimes, we're just reacting.

For many reasons, we can find ourselves using coping behaviors we thought we had outgrown. We start neglecting ourselves, taking care of others, feeling victimized, freezing feelings, overreacting, and trying to control. We begin to feel dependent and needy, guilty, afraid, obligated, depressed, deprived, undeserving, and trapped. The codependent crazies come back, and we feel neck-deep in shame.

No need to feel shame. I've questioned thousands of recovering people. No one claimed a perfect recovery.

From "Recycling: The Relapse Process"
by Melody Beattie

TALK, TRUST, AND FEEL

Keeping Codependency Out of Your Life

Melody Beattie, Veronica Ray,
Brian DesRoches,
Roseann Lloyd,
Jennifer Schneider,
Stephanie Abbott,
John Hough and Marshall Hardy,
and Brenda Schaeffer

A Hazelden Book
BALLANTINE BOOKS • NEW YORK

Editor's note:

Hazelden Educational Materials offers a variety of information on chemical dependency and related areas. Our publications do not necessarily represent Hazelden's programs, nor do they officially speak for any Twelve Step organization.

In all cases, the names of people and the circumstances of stories described in this book have been changed to protect anonymity.

The following publishers have generally given permission to use quotations from copyrighted works: From *Al-Anon Faces Alcoholism*, copyright © 1986, by Al-Anon Family Group Headquarters, Inc. Reprinted by permission of Al-Anon Family Group Headquarters, Inc. From *One Day at a Time in Al-Anon*, copyright © 1973, by Al-Anon Family Group Headquarters, Inc. Reprinted by permission of Al-Anon Family Group Headquarters, Inc. From *Alcoholics Anonymous*, copyright © 1976, by A.A. World Services, Inc. Reprinted by permission of A.A. World Services, Inc.

Library of Congress Catalog Card Number: 91-65853

ISBN 0-345-37455-X

This edition published by arrangement with the Hazelden Foundation

Manufactured in the United States of America

First Ballantine Books Edition: December 1991

CONTENTS

INTRODUCTION

The concept of codependency is the core of a movement that defines and explains the pain that many people feel. This pain comes from not being able to take care of ourselves while trying so hard to take care of others. The hurt comes from overworking, overcaretaking, oversacrificing, while something in us is tired, hungry, needy, and never taken care of. We are sick and tired and not going to take it anymore, if we can only figure out what "it" is! And we will, because there are things we can do that will make recovery happen—as the various writers in this book point out.

There seem to be as many theories about codependency as there are writers; the word itself is too new for dictionaries. The definitions have evolved from the word *co-alcoholic,* which initially meant someone whose life and personality had been affected by someone else's alcoholism. *Codependent* behavior can refer to the dynamics in an important relationship with any kind of addict. It can also refer to a certain learned pattern of behavior in relationships, a pattern that ultimately brings us pain.

Some writers have defined *codependency* as a primary disease (an ongoing, progressive disease that gets worse and worse if not taken care of). But others believe it is a result of prolonged traumatic stress that can happen to a healthy personality. Some theorists enlarge the definition to include people not necessarily affected by someone else's addiction, but who have been raised in families with rigid, oppressive rules.

These rules can discourage expression of feelings and discussion of problems, put an unhealthy emphasis on control of oneself and of others, and produce strong feelings of shame and guilt. Claudia Black summarized these rules best when she said, "Don't talk, don't feel, don't trust."

I believe *codependency* is a collection of traits that can make us miserable if we have enough of them, and some of them are encouraged by the society we live in. These traits include

- trying to control others
- trying to help and understand others while ignoring our own needs
- confusing our responsibilities with those of others
- repressing feelings
- being emotionally involved with addicts (such as gamblers, alcoholics, or sex addicts)
- believing that our self-worth is based on *how someone else behaves*

Codependency is like a mirror. We see ourselves reflected in someone else: our needs, our worth, our ambition, our security, and our hopes are all projected onto other people. Until we learn to focus on ourselves and develop our own strong identities, we'll probably continue trying to manage and direct the lives of others.

Probably no one has all of the codependent traits I've described, since some of them may be to some extent contradictory. Still, the presence of even a few of these traits can destroy serenity and make sane relationships impossible. The one point all the theorists agree on is this: codependency (by whatever name) is a relationship problem.

In this book you'll read about how you can start healing your relationships or bolster the growth you've already realized. The featured authors represent some of the best voices in the recovery movement as they offer insight into how we can become people who talk, trust, and feel.

Stephanie Abbott
President, National Foundation
for Alcoholism Communications

RECYCLING:
THE RELAPSE PROCESS

Melody Beattie

"I did it again," Jan confided. "And I did it ten years after I began my recovery from codependency.

"Steve and I are divorced. He hasn't paid child support in six months because he's drinking and not working, and I handed him two hundred and fifty dollars of my hard-earned money—probably to get drunk on.

"I'm furious! I can't believe I let him do that to me. I know better. I didn't want to do it. I let him bully and guilt me out of the money."

Jan took a deep breath and continued. "Afterward, I drove over to his apartment and demanded the money back. I made a fool of myself, screaming and stomping around.

"I feel angry, depressed, and ashamed. Sometimes I

Reprinted, with changes, with permission of Hazelden Foundation. From *Beyond Codependency: And Getting Better All the Time*, by Melody Beattie. Copyright © 1989 by Hazelden Foundation.

think I don't know anything about recovery. I called my sponsor and whined to her. All those meetings! All that therapy! All that work! Didn't it mean anything? I was still caretaking. Still allowing people to use me. And still stomping around acting crazy.''

I asked Jan what her sponsor said. ''She said at least I was asking why I was allowing people to use me, instead of asking why they were doing this to me,'' Jan said. ''And she said at least I could recognize when my behavior was crazy.''

Over the years, I've seen people use different diagrams to represent the recovery or growth process. I've seen recovery portrayed as a zigzagging line moving upward and forward, with each zig forming a higher peak than the last. (See Diagram 1, page 7.)* I've seen recovery drawn as a circular line moving inward in smaller circles until an inner core of stability is reached; an inner core large enough to permit continued growth. (See Diagram 2.)** I've seen recovery diagramed as a line moving upward and forward, making repetitively spinning circles on the way, cyclical but forward-moving. (See Diagram 3.)† One diagram I haven't seen drawn to represent recovery is a straight line upward and forward. (See Diagram 4.) Recovery is not this.

Recovery is a process. Within that process is another one called relapse. Regression, reverting, slips—

---

* This is a diagram often used to represent recovery from chemical addiction, recovery from codependency, and recovery and growth.
** Scott Egleston and others have used this to diagram codependency and recovery.
† Lonny Owen used this to diagram recovery from codependency. He got the idea from someone else, who got the idea from another. . . .

whatever we call it, any diagram we use to represent growth needs to accommodate it.

In spite of our best efforts to stay on track, we sometimes find ourselves reverting to old ways of thinking, feeling, and behaving, even when we know better.

Relapse can sneak up on us, linger, and become as confusing as our original codependency. Or it can be brief. Sometimes, we're reacting to other people's craziness. Sometimes, we're reacting to ourselves. Sometimes, we're reacting to the years of training we've had in how to be codependent. Sometimes, we're just reacting.

For many reasons, we can find ourselves using coping behaviors we thought we had outgrown. We start neglecting ourselves, taking care of others, feeling victimized, freezing feelings, overreacting, and trying to control. We begin to feel dependent and needy, guilty, afraid, obligated, depressed, deprived, undeserving, and trapped. The codependent crazies come back, and we feel neck-deep in shame.

No need to feel shame. I've questioned thousands of recovering people. No one claimed a perfect recovery.

Diagram 1

Diagram 2

Diagram 3

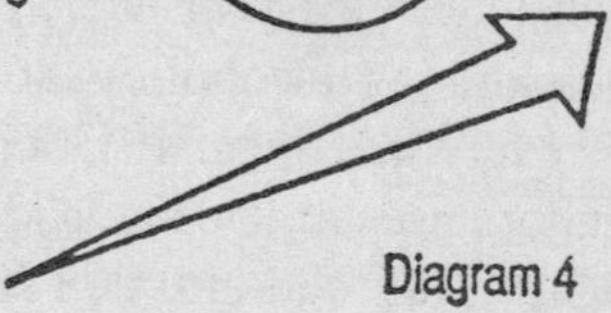

Diagram 4

*   *   *

"I thought something awful was wrong with me," recalls Charlene. "I kept threatening to leave my boyfriend, but I didn't leave him. I felt disconnected from people—all alone in the world. I got irritable, depressed, and couldn't sleep. I thought I was dying. I went to the doctor. He said I was fine, but I didn't feel fine. This went on for months before I realized it was my codependency. I got really scared. It took some work, but now I'm back on track again."

Jack tells this story: "Last weekend my friend's wife called me. I'm recovering from chemical addiction and codependency. My friend is still drinking, and his wife is still thinking about going to Al-Anon. She planned to leave town for the weekend and asked me to stay with her husband while she was gone. She said *he* really wanted to stay sober that weekend and *he* wanted to go fishing with me. I agreed. When I arrived, I realized her husband had no intention of going fishing. He wanted to go drinking. She set me up to be his baby-sitter for the weekend. I felt tricked and trapped. It was one of the most miserable weekends I've had in my two years of recovery. And I couldn't open my mouth and get out. I had a big slip, a codependency slip."

Marilyn tells this story: "I had been recovering for five years when I moved in with Bob, a recovering alcoholic. One year later, I found myself living with a nondrinking alcoholic who had stopped attending his recovery meetings. I started feeling crazy again. I felt guilty, insecure, needy, and resentful. It happened gradually. I just slid into it. I stopped setting boundaries. I quit asking for what I wanted and needed. I stopped saying, 'No!' I stopped taking care of myself. I couldn't figure out what was wrong. Then one day, when I was considering ending the relationship, I found myself thinking, *No! I can't do that. I can't live without him.* That thought jolted me into awareness and action. I know better than that!''

Relapse happens to many of us. Relapse happens to people who have been recovering for ten months or ten years. It happens not because we're deficient or lackadaisical. Relapse happens because it's a normal part of the recovery process.

In fact, it's so normal I'm not going to call it "relapse." I'm going to call it "recycling."*

Relapse, according to the New World Dictionary, means to slip or fall back into a former condition after improvement or *seeming* improvement.** *Recycle* means to recover; or to pass through a cycle or part of a cycle again for checking or treating.†

" 'Relapse' sounds like going all the way back to where we started from—square one on the game board," explains my friend, Scott Egleston, who is a therapist. "We don't go all the way back. When we finish a recycling process, we move to a progressed location on our recovery journey."

Recycling is more than a normal part of recovery. Sometimes, it's a necessary part. For example, in the beginning of this chapter, Jan talked about allowing her ex-husband to bully her out of money. Her story has an

---

* Scott Egleston suggested this term.
** *New World Dictionary of the American Language, Second College Edition* (New York: Simon & Schuster, Inc., 1984), 1198.
† *New World Dictionary of the American Language, Second College Edition* (New York: Simon & Schuster, Inc., 1984), 1189.

epilogue. About four months after the incident, Jan was having coffee with her sponsor. Her sponsor asked Jan if she had learned anything from the incident.

"By then, I had learned something from it," Jan said, "something valuable. That incident was part of a larger, important lesson I was in the midst of learning. Financially, I was finally getting on my feet, and I was starting to leave behind the sick people in my life. I was standing up to the bullying, and I was letting go of the guilt about becoming healthy. The lesson I was learning involved the idea that I could feel compassion for people without acting on it."

All our recycling incidents can have epilogues. We can gain from them when they happen. Recycling is a chance to do our recovery work. It's a way to discover what we need to work on and work through. It's one way we figure out what we haven't yet learned, so we can start to learn that. It's a way to solidify what we've already learned, so we continue to know that. Recycling is about learning our lessons so we can move forward on our journey.

Activity
1. What would a diagram of your recovery look like?
2. As you progress through this book, you may want to start accumulating a list of affirmations. Some suggestions for affirmations on recycling would be:

• My recovery history is okay. All my experiences are necessary and valuable.
• I am learning what I need to know. I will learn what I need to when the time is right.
• I am right where I need to be.

COMMON RECYCLING SITUATIONS

Recycling on the Job

We can recycle at work for many reasons. Sometimes, we bring our behaviors with us. If we're still trying to control people at home, we may be doing the same at work. If we're not setting boundaries at home, we may not be doing it at work either. Sometimes, we've acquired self-care skills at home and in personal relationships, but we haven't learned how to take care of ourselves on the job and in professional relationships.

Other times, issues at work can point to a larger issue we need to address. "I haven't been happy about my job," says Alice, who has been recovering from codependency for many years. "I've been complaining and whining about it. So I decided to go see a counselor, and during counseling a new awareness struck me.

"I don't like my job. I took it because it met my parents' standards. I've stayed because they wouldn't approve of me leaving. I can hear them: 'All those benefits? All that seniority? You're going to walk away and leave all that?'

"Yes," Alice says, "that's exactly what I'm going to do."

Sometimes, we find ourselves working with an alcoholic or other troubled person. An addicted person can inflict as much chaos at work as he or she can at home.

When a prestigious hospital offered Marlyss a job, she was delighted. She had put herself through nursing school in mid-life. Eight years ago, she began recovering from codependency, and developing her career was a big part of that. But two and a half years after she started working at the hospital, Marlyss was feeling crazy again.

"I finally figured out what was happening," she says. "I had been promoted to a supervisory position. My supervisor was a practicing alcoholic. The nurses under my supervision were reacting to my alcoholic supervisor and the crazy system. I was reacting to everyone—my supervisor and the nurses I supervised. I was in my familiar role of peacemaker and caretaker, feeling responsible for everyone and everything. It was like the family system at home used to be. And I felt like I used to—real codependent."

Marlyss began to practice detachment at work. After a while, she found a different job. She's worked there three years now. "I love it," Marlyss says. "Moving on was one of the best moves I ever made."

Some people may find themselves employed by abusive or abrasive people. "My boss treated me so nasty," Ella says. "He was verbally abusive. He made sexual innuendos. I had been recovering from codependency for several years, and it still took me months to realize I wasn't doing something wrong, he was."

Jerry, a recovering codependent and alcoholic who owned his own business, had the following experience. "I hired a secretary. She was great, at first," Jerry recalls. "She was willing to learn and work hard. Before long, I discovered she was married to an alcoholic. At first I felt sorry for her, then I got mad. Whenever he was doing too much drinking, she didn't want to stay home. She worked late and weekends, and charged me overtime. It was taking her longer than it should to get her work done. She was making a lot of mistakes at my expense.

"I didn't say much at first. I suggested she go to Al-Anon, but she wasn't ready. I felt ashamed about getting angry. She really did have it hard, being married to an alcoholic. But I could also see how she kept setting herself up to be used by the guy. I got angrier and angrier, then the pieces started to fit. I've stopped feeling sorry for her and started taking care of myself. I know it's a myth that codependents are sicker than alcoholics. I know how much codependents hurt; I am one. But I'm also beginning to see how difficult it can be to deal with one. You can get just as codependent on a codependent as you can on an alcoholic."

A family is a system with its own rules, roles, and personality. And employment settings can be similar. Sometimes, a person in that system is dysfunctional. Sometimes, the system is dysfunctional, either covertly or overtly.

"I had been recovering for about two years when I went to work for a radio station," says Al, an adult child of an alcoholic. "I really wanted the job. I still do. But boy, did it hook my codependency. We're a small station on a small budget with a small staff and a large mission—doing all we can to save the city.

"After I'd been working there a couple of months, I noticed many of my codependency symptoms reappearing. This time it wasn't about my relationship; it was about my job. I was working sixty hours a week, neglecting myself, feeling like no matter how much I did it wasn't enough. I was feeling irritable, angry, and guilty because I couldn't do more. Whenever I considered setting boundaries or taking care of myself, I felt more guilt. How could I be so selfish? Who would do it, if I didn't? What about our mission? There wasn't enough of me to go around. Now, I'm figuring out how to take care of myself in this organization.''

Sally found herself in a difficult employment situation. She took a management position in a sales force several years after beginning recovery from chemical dependency and codependency. Within six months, she started feeling ''nuts'' again. ''Just like in the old days,'' Sally says.

''Company policy surpassed high-pressure selling. It involved unethical practices. The company used people—employees and customers. I didn't feel comfortable following company policy. For a while, I tried to pretend I did. Then, pretending got too hard. I talked to my supervisor. He understood, but company policy was company policy. By then, I had learned you can't change other people. Now, I was learning you can't change a corporation either. The only thing left was to change myself. I did. I changed jobs.''

For years, Earnie Larsen, a respected author and lecturer on recovery issues, has preached that some systems demand sick behavior from the people in them. He was talking about families, but employment systems can be just as demanding.

Sometimes, recycling at work is a clue to something we need to work on or through. Other times, it's an indicator of how much we've grown. We often choose relationships that are about as healthy as we are and meet our current (but changing) needs; we often choose jobs in the same way. We can grow out of relationships; we can grow out of jobs.

"I took a job during the first year of my recovery from codependency," Kelly says. "I was devastated at the time, crushed by a sick relationship that had gone on for years. At first, the job felt good. It was a safe place to be. The work wasn't demanding, but it kept me busy. And the people were nice. I felt like I fit in."

After about eighteen months, Kelly's feelings about her job changed. She felt out of place. She started repressing feelings, going numb at work.

"I don't know how or when it happened, but I realized I no longer fit in. The healthier I became, the more I saw many of my co-workers were victims. And they wanted me to be a victim. As I grew and did more things to take care of myself, they got angry at me. I felt torn. I wanted to fit in and be part of the crowd. But I didn't want to be a victim."

Although Kelly has decided to stay at her job for a while, she says she suspects she'll soon move on. She's been recovering long enough to know change isn't necessarily bad. It can bring us to our next plateau of growth.

Other systems besides employment settings can invite us to behave codependently. We can recycle at church, in recovery groups, and in social, professional, or charitable associations. Wherever people gather, the possibility of us using our codependent coping behaviors exists.

"I went to church on Sunday feeling good. I left feeling ashamed. I never felt good enough, no matter what I did," says Len, a recovering codependent. "I constantly felt pressured into volunteering for things. I couldn't tell if I was giving money because I wanted to or because I felt guilty. I was fine all week. But I felt crazy in church.

"I've since switched churches. I need to hear God loves me, not that He's waiting to punish me. I've lived with fear and condemnation all my life. Looking back, I think that church was as shame-based as my family. I just didn't realize it until I got healthier."

We can recycle in therapy or support groups, too. "I knew I was an alcoholic and needed A.A. I also knew I was codependent and needed Al-Anon," says Theresa. "But members of my A.A. group started giving me a hard time. They said if I was really working a good A.A. program, I wouldn't need Al-Anon.

"I dropped out of Al-Anon, and started feeling real crazy again. Then I realized the people in my A.A. group didn't have to approve of me dealing with my codependency. Either they didn't understand, or they were uncomfortable with my attendance in Al-Anon. I didn't need to figure them out; my job was to take care of myself."

Taking care of ourselves may mean finding another job, church, or group. Or, it may mean figuring out how to function in the job, church, or group we're in. Theresa has continued attending the same A.A. group. She also continues to attend Al-Anon.

Recycling in Relationships

Recycling is possible and fairly predictable in any relationship. We can give up our power and get crazy with people we've known for years and with strangers. We can start reacting to people we love and people we're not certain we like.

We can start feeling guilty, as if we are at fault, when others behave inappropriately. Sometimes, we recycle without any help from them at all.

Sometimes we need to learn to use certain recovery skills that we've acquired in one kind of relationship, such as our special love relationship, in another kind of relationship, such as a friendship.

"I can set boundaries with my husband and children. I'm lousy at setting boundaries with friends," says one woman.

We can react to new people in our lives—people whose addiction or problem catches us off-guard. Or we can react to people whose addiction or dysfunction we know all too well.

"I can be going along just fine," says Sarah. "But after ten minutes on the phone with my ex-husband, I'm a basket case again. I still try to trust him. I still go into denial about his alcoholism. I still get hooked into shame and guilt when I talk to him. It's taken me a long time, but I'm finally learning I don't have to talk to him. The same thing happens each time."

Sometimes, past relationships hold important lessons. We may need to go back long enough to realize we don't want to stay.

Family reunions, holidays, and other family gatherings can challenge our recovery. Besides triggering a reaction to whatever is happening that day, it can trigger old feelings.

Dealing with family members, whether they're in

recovery or not, can be provocative. "I get trapped on the phone with family members," explains Linda. "I can feel myself going through the whole process, feeling enraged, guilty, then going numb. They're not in recovery. They go on and on. I tell them I have to go, but they don't listen. Short of hanging up, I don't know what to do!

"Sometimes it leaves me feeling drained for hours. I get so angry. My family is important to me. I'd like to tape record those conversations and make them listen to themselves for endless hours, like I do.

"I've been recovering from codependency for eight years. I know the answer isn't making other people listen to themselves and 'see the light.' The solution is me listening to myself and me 'seeing the light.' Sometimes I can cope with my family, but sometimes, I still get tangled up with them."

We may find ourselves periodically, or cyclically, reacting to certain people in our lives. "I've noticed my recycling in relationships comes in cycles. I'm fine for a few months, then it feels like crazy people come crawling out of the woodwork. It's usually the same people, and they seem determined to inflict their insanity on me, all at the same time," says one woman. "I don't understand it. But I do understand this: it becomes time to detach and take care of myself."

Dealing with children can challenge our recovery. "I'm good at taking care of myself with the rest of the world. But with my kids, I feel guilty when I say no. I feel guilty when I feel angry at them. I feel guilty about disciplining them. I allow them to treat me terribly, then I'm the one who feels guilty!" says another woman.

"My son has admitted he deliberately uses guilt-producing tactics on me. In his weaker moments, he calls it 'the guilt trap.' He's admitted he compares me to other mothers, and lies about what they're letting their kids do, to control me. My kids know what they're doing. It's about time I learn what I need to do," she concludes.

"Setting boundaries with my children is harder for me than setting limits at work, with friends, or with my girlfriend," says a divorced man. "I feel so guilty when I do, and so victimized when I don't."

Dealing with other people's children can be more difficult than dealing with our own. I've asked recovering people, "What's the hardest part of your relationship?" Many people in relationships involving children from past marriages say, "Dealing with the children."

But the greatest challenge to our recoveries still seems to be our special love relationships. "I don't know how to be in love and not be codependent," says a recovering woman. "I was friends for over a year with a man. The minute we moved in together, we both stopped taking care of ourselves and tried to control each other. It really got nuts. When I'm in love, anything goes. And what usually goes first is my recovery behaviors."

We can get uncomfortable when a relationship gets too close and too good. Crisis and chaos may not feel good, but they can feel comfortable. Sometimes, we get so anxious waiting for the formidable other shoe to drop that we take it off and toss it ourselves.

"I'm in a good relationship, one with tremendous potential," says a recovering woman. "We get along great, but whenever things get too good, I create a problem. At first, I couldn't see this was my pattern. I thought things just got good, then bad. Now, I'm starting to see my part."

There are many reasons for recycling in relationships. Sometimes the relationship is over, but we're not ready to end it. Sometimes the relationship needs to be enjoyed, but we're too frightened to do that. Sometimes we're making chaos to avoid intimacy. Sometimes falling in love can resemble codependency; as boundaries weaken, we focus on the other person and have a sense of loss of control. Sometimes what we call "codependent behaviors" are a normal part of intimate or close relationships.

Relationships are where we take our recovery show on the road. Taking good care of ourselves doesn't mean we avoid relationships. The goal of recovery is learning how to function in relationships. The task during recycling is to relax and let ourselves learn whatever we need to learn.

Other Recycling Situations

Many other circumstances can provoke our codependency. Sometimes we begin denying that codependency is real and recovery is our responsibility. We may neglect our recoveries and stop taking care of ourselves. Sometimes we neglect ourselves before a recycling incident; sometimes we do it after we begin recycling, making things worse.

"How long do I need to keep working at recovery?" asks one woman. "All my life, I guess," she says, answering her own question. "Whenever I stop taking my recovery seriously, my life gets crazy again."

Sometimes our old reactions appear for *no reason*.

Sometimes recycling is part of the experimental process we go through as we struggle to acquire new behaviors and shed old, self-defeating ones.

Getting sick or becoming overly tired can trigger codependent reactions in us. Stress—from today and yesterday—can trigger our codependency. Our instinctive reaction to stressful situations can be to neglect ourselves.

Innocuous events that remind us of past traumatic events can also trigger our codependency. Triggers remind our subconscious of a traumatic event, causing codependent feelings and behaviors to emerge. This can include

- feeling anxious or afraid
- freezing feelings, or "going numb"
- "focusing on others and neglecting ourselves
- attempting to control things, events, and people
- experiencing sudden low self-worth
- any of the codependent behaviors or feelings we did or felt during the actual event

We automatically start reacting and protecting ourselves.

We each have our own triggers. If it was connected to something frightening or distressing that happened before, it can be a trigger now.

Almost anything can be a trigger:

- conflict
- the threat of someone leaving us, even if we want him or her to leave
- confrontation
- paying bills
- hearing a certain song

Anything connected with, resembling, or representing a past traumatic experience can be a trigger. Falling in love can resemble codependency; it can trigger it, too.

Understanding our triggers may not make these sudden resurgences of codependency disappear, but understanding can help us get out more swiftly.

"Paying bills is a trigger for me," says Carol. "I've got enough money now. That's not the problem. The problem is all the years I was married to an alcoholic, and there wasn't enough money. Before I learned about my triggers, I felt anxious and distressed the day I paid the bills. Now, I recognize what's happening. I still get skittish, but I tell myself it's okay. There's enough money now. And there's going to be enough."

Problems and trauma aren't the only matters that can provoke codependency. Success, in any area of our lives, can cause us to start controlling and caretaking again.

"I know how to cope with emergencies, tragedy, and disappointment," confides a recovering woman. "I don't know how to deal with success, peace, and loving relationships. Those things are uncomfortable. I get scared. I wonder what bad thing is going to happen next. Some terrible thing always did in the past. It's difficult for me to believe I deserve good things. It's even harder for me to believe good things can last."

Changing circumstances can cause us to recycle. Changing jobs, moving, ending a relationship, the threat of ending a relationship, a change in finances, or a shift in routine can be unnerving. Even desirable change brings a sense of loss. Most of us have been through so much change and loss that we don't want to go through any more.

About six months after *Codependent No More* was released, my life began to change. I was working for a newspaper and doing free-lance writing on weekends and evenings. Requests for me to speak began filtering in. I was shuffling all this into the routine of being the single parent of two young children. I was also trying to stay involved in my own recovery process and find time to have fun.

My life kept filling up with new activities. I kept trying to hang on to the old ones and make room for the new. I kept waiting for things to go back to normal. What I didn't realize was that "normal" had changed.

Then I got sick with double pneumonia. I learned of the diagnosis twenty-four hours before I was scheduled to speak in Joplin, Missouri. I thought it would be inappropriate to cancel that close to the event, so I pushed myself through. When I returned to Minnesota, I had several stories due at the paper. I told myself I couldn't cancel those either.

I spent a day struggling to grind out a story that ordinarily would have taken me three hours. After eight hours, I hadn't yet produced the first paragraph. I stayed late, hoping the quiet would help me think more clearly. By eight o'clock that night, I had wrestled out four or five paragraphs.

When I went to the lounge to take a break, I heard that still voice within me. It said: *It's time to take care of yourself*. I was running around the country, preaching those words. I had written a book carrying that message. Now, it was time to listen to myself.

When we start feeling the codependent crazies again, we know what time it is. It's time to take care of ourselves.

Whether we recycle or not, we can benefit by putting extra attention into self-care during these circumstances. And whether we're reacting to a crazy system, a person, ourselves, our pasts, or just reacting, taking care of ourselves remains a "no-fault" issue. It's our responsibility.

Somewhere between our first response, shaking our finger at the other person and saying, "It's your fault," and our second reaction, pointing that finger at ourselves and wondering, *What's wrong with me?*—there's a lesson to learn. That lesson is ours to learn.

Activity

1. Did any recycling incidents come to mind as you read this chapter? How did you take care of yourself in that situation?
2. Do any people in your life seem to particularly trigger your codependency? Who? What happens? What are some ways you can start taking care of yourself with these people?
3. As you go through your daily routine, watch for

your "triggers." What things seem to engage those old codependent feelings "for no reason"? Look for the reason, the connection to the past. When that happens, what can you tell yourself to help yourself feel better?

GETTING THROUGH THE CYCLE

Recycling can mean a momentary lapse into our old behaviors. Or recycling can lead to more serious problems: depression, use of mood-altering chemicals to cope, or physical illness. Codependency is progressive; recycling can be, too. We can get stuck, spin our wheels, then discover we've gotten ourselves more deeply entrenched in the muck.

Whether our recycling experience lasts six minutes or six months, our instinctive reaction is usually one of denial, shame, and self-neglect. That's not the way out. That's the way in more deeply.

We get out of, or through, a recycling process by practicing acceptance, self-compassion, and self-care. These attitudes and behaviors may not come as effortlessly as denial, shame, and neglect. We've spent years practicing denial, shame, and neglect. But we can learn to practice healthier alternatives, even when it feels awkward. Some suggestions for doing that follow.

Recycling Myths
Believing any of the following myths about recycling may make recovery more difficult than necessary.

• I should be further along than I am.

- If I've been recovering for a number of years, I shouldn't be having problems with this anymore.
- If I was working a good program, I wouldn't be doing this.
- If I'm a professional in the recovery, mental health, or general helping field, I shouldn't be having this problem.
- If my recovery was real, I wouldn't be doing this.
- People wouldn't respect me if they knew I thought, felt, or did this.
- Once changed, a behavior is gone forever.
- I couldn't possibly be doing this again. I know better.
- Oh, no! I'm back to square one.

These are myths. If we believe them, we need to try to change what we believe. It's okay to have problems. It's okay to recycle. People who work good programs and have good recoveries recycle, even if they're professionals. It's okay to do "it" again, even when we know better. We haven't gone all the way back to square one. Who knows? We may learn from it this time.

If we insist on blaming or feeling ashamed, we can give ourselves a limited time to do that. Five to fifteen minutes should be enough.

Taking Care of Ourselves

After we've accepted ourselves and given ourselves a hug, we ask ourselves two questions.

- "What do I need to do to take care of myself?"
- "What am I supposed to learn?"

Often, the self-care concepts we need to practice are basic:

- acceptance
- surrender
- realistic evaluation of what we can control
- detachment
- removing the victim
- dealing with feelings
- taking what we want and need seriously
- setting boundaries
- making choices and taking responsibility for them
- setting goals
- getting honest
- letting go
- giving ourselves huge doses of love and nurturing

Consciously focusing on our recovery program, talking to healthy people, plying ourselves with meditations and positive thoughts, relaxing, and doing fun activities help, too.

We need to get our balance back.

Taking care of ourselves at work may require some different considerations than caring for ourselves at home. Certain behaviors may be appropriate at home but could result in loss of our job. We may not want to tell the boss how mad we are at him. Self-care is self-responsibility.

Codependency is a self-defeating cycle. Codependent feelings lead to self-neglect, self-neglect leads to more codependent feelings and behaviors, leading to more self-neglect, and around we go. Recovery is a more energizing cycle. Self-care leads to better feelings, healthier feelings lead to more self-care, and around that track we travel.

I don't know precisely what you need to do to take care of yourself. But I know you can figure it out.

Another thing I don't know is what lesson you're learning. It's all I can do to learn my own. I can't tell you how to make sense of the particular experiences in your life, but I can tell you this: between you and your Higher Power, you will figure that out, too.

Recycling Tips

Although I don't have a formula for self-care and learning life's lessons, I've collected some tips that may help during recycling.

- If it feels crazy, it probably is. Often when we run into a crazy system, our first reaction is still to wonder what's wrong with us. We can trust some people, but we can't trust everyone. We can trust ourselves.
- If we're protecting ourselves, something may be threatening us. Maybe a trigger is reminding us of the old days or an old message is sabotaging us. Sometimes, someone in our present is threatening us, and we're trying to pretend they're not. If we're protecting ourselves, it helps to understand who or what is scaring us, and what we're protecting ourselves from.
- When one method of problem solving fails, try another. Sometimes, we get stuck. We encounter a problem, decide to solve it a certain way, fail, then repeatedly, sometimes for years, try to solve that problem in the same way, even though that way doesn't work. Regroup and try something else.

- Self-will doesn't work any better during recovery than it did before. Surrendering does work. Sometimes in recycling, we're going through the process of denying a problem that's creeping into our awareness. We're struggling to avoid it or overcome it by exerting greater amounts of self-will. When self-will fails, try surrender.

- Feelings of guilt, pity, and obligation are to the codependent what the first drink is to the alcoholic. Watch out for what happens next.

- Feeling sad and frustrated because we can't control someone or something is not the same as controlling.*

- Trying to recoup our losses generally doesn't work. "If I look back and stare at my losses too long, they gain on me," says one man. "I've learned to take them and run."

- We cannot simultaneously set a boundary and take care of the other person's feelings.**

- Today isn't yesterday. Things change.

- We don't have to do more today than we can reasonably do. If we're tired, rest. If we need to play, play. The work will get done.

- When depressed, look to see if anger, shame, or guilt are present.†

---

* This is wisdom from Scott Egleston.

** I got this wisdom from a woman I met at an airport. I neglected to get her name, but she travels across the country teaching nurses about codependency, bases much of her teaching on *Codependent No More*, and shared this tidbit with me.

† Based in part on information in *Here Comes the Sun*, Gayle Rosellini and Mark Worden (Center City, Minn.: Hazelden Educational Materials, 1987).

- If we're not certain, we can wait.
- It's hard to feel compassion for someone while that person is using or victimizing us. We'll probably feel angry. First, we stop allowing ourselves to be used. Then, we work toward compassion. Anger can motivate us to set boundaries, but we don't need to stay resentful to keep taking care of ourselves.
- If we listen to ourselves, we'll probably hear ourselves say what the problem is. The next step is acceptance.
- We never outgrow our need for nurturing and self-care.
- If everything looks black, we've probably got our eyes shut.

When all else fails, try gratitude. Sometimes, that's what we're supposed to be learning. If we can't think of anything to be grateful about, be grateful anyway. Will gratitude. Fake it if necessary. Sometimes in recycling, we need to change something we're doing. Sometimes things are being worked out in us, important intangibles that may not be clear for months or years, things like patience, faith, and self-esteem.

"I've had a lot of ups and downs, a lot of pain, and a lot of loss," says one woman. "I'm still not sure what everything's been about, but I've learned a few things. I've learned that where I live, what I wear, and where I work isn't me. I'm me. And no matter what happens, I can land on my feet."

Come to think of it, maybe we shouldn't call relapse "recycling." Maybe we should call it "cycles of growth." Or maybe we should just call it "growth."

Recycling, getting stuck, bad days, whatever we call it, can be tough, especially if we've had a taste of better days. We can frighten ourselves, worrying that all the old stuff is back again, maybe to stay. We don't have to worry. We don't have to go all the way back. The old stuff isn't here to stay. It's part of the process, and in that process, some days go better than others. We can count them all for joy.

Activity

1. What are your patterns of self-neglect when you get into a recycling situation? For example, mine include: eliminating fun activities, neglecting proper nutrition, and pushing harder when the problem is I've pushed too hard.

2. What are some of your favorite acts of self-care, activities what help you feel good about yourself? What are some things you enjoyed doing for yourself when you began your recovery from codependency that you've stopped doing? What is your rationale for not doing those things anymore?*

* This came from Lonny Owen.

THE ELEMENTS OF RECOVERY

Jennifer P. Schneider, M.D.

The self-help groups that are best suited to promoting recovery from codependency are those that teach the Twelve Step program. These groups (free of cost to join) meet weekly in thousands of locations across the country. Based on the Twelve Steps of A.A., there are now also groups that address narcotic abuse, compulsive overeating, compulsive spending, compulsive gambling, and compulsive sexual behaviors. There are also support groups for spouses and significant others of people struggling with these compulsive behaviors that function similarly to Al-Anon, the Twelve Step group for family and friends of alcoholics.

None of these groups provides professional counseling; they are gatherings of people who have experienced the same problem and who have come together to share their experience, strength, and hope with each other. Experience has shown that hearing what has worked for someone who has been in the same situation is a strong stimulus for change.

The Twelve Step program is a deceptively simple path to recovery, originating fifty years ago by the founders of Alcoholics Anonymous. The program consists of three elements essential to making changes. The first is recognizing that our life is intolerable as is, and that change is necessary. The second element is deciding to do whatever it takes to implement the change, and the third element is acting to bring about the change.

The Steps are the basic tools of the program. The first three are belief Steps, and the last nine are action Steps. In brief, the program consists of recognizing we cannot solve our problems alone; believing that an outside force (a Higher Power) can help us; admitting our problems and character defects to ourselves and confessing them to another person; making restitution for our wrongdoing wherever possible; monitoring our thoughts and behavior on an ongoing basis; continuing to seek spiritual assistance in dealing with our problems; and letting other people who need the same kind of help know about the program.

Step One, as applied to sexual addiction, states, "We admitted we were powerless over compulsive sexual behavior and that our lives had become unmanageable."* For the coaddict this means we are powerless

---

* The Steps quoted in "The Elements of Recovery" are reprinted with permission of Alcoholics Anonymous World Services, Inc. The full

over someone else's sexual behavior. One woman described what Step One meant to her when she first encountered it.

> When my husband first joined a self-help group for sexual addiction, he suggested that I go to Al-Anon for my own recovery. I didn't think there was any reason for me to go—after all, he was the one with the problem! But like the good coaddict that I was, I went in order to please him. What I heard at the first meeting made so much sense that I can still remember the impact it had on me. The topic was powerlessness over the addict. Until then, I hadn't realized I was powerless over my husband. On the contrary, I had been running my life for years on the principle that I had a great deal of power over him, although of course I hadn't realized I believed this. I continually tried to keep my children on their best behavior because I thought it would keep him from getting angry. I tried to stay slim and dressed becomingly so he wouldn't want to look at other women. I didn't confront him with my suspicions and fears. And when, despite my best efforts, his moods would swing like a pendulum, I analyzed what I might have done to cause this and what I could have done differently to prevent it. I would review what he had said to me and what I had said to him, and would plan what I might say to him next time the same situation arose. I devoted an enormous amount of emotional energy trying to please him,

Twelve Steps of Alcoholics Anonymous appear in Appendix 1. The full Twelve Steps of Al-Anon appear in Appendix 2.

to understand him, and to prevent his recurrent unhappiness, resentment, and complaints of boredom with our marriage. And when my efforts did not succeed, I thought I just needed to try harder.

At Al-Anon, I realized how useless my efforts had been and how powerless I really was over his behavior. I learned that his craziness was not a response to me; it was a response to his addiction and to how he felt about himself. To my surprise, with the acceptance of powerlessness came a tremendous feeling of relief. I realized that I could relinquish the terrible sense of responsibility that I had felt until then for my husband's happiness and the blame that I had felt for his failures and his unhappiness. I believed I was responsible for his happiness; this was the core of my fruitless efforts and my obsession with him. To accept my powerlessness meant to give up that awesome responsibility. From now on I need to be responsible only for my own happiness. An enormous burden was lifted from my shoulders that first evening at Al-Anon: the burden of responsibility for another person's happiness. This is the powerful message of Step One, which to me was so freeing.

Other coaddicts have expressed the same feelings when they understood Step One. The wife of a cocaine addict who had multiple affairs said:

I just found out this week that I'm a real person. I had hooked onto him as though we were Siamese twins. Now I feel a tremendous relief because I'm responsible only for myself and not for him. It's up to

*him whether he wants to be in the program, and then
I'll have to make my decision about staying with him.*

A consequence of Step One is our ability to detach
from a person or a problem. Detachment is a much
misunderstood concept. It does not mean we do not
care or we are washing our hands of the person. It
means we recognize that we cannot solve another person's problems for him, and worrying about the situation will not bring about change. Learning to detach
allows us to love without going crazy. It allows us to
assess realistically what we can change and what we
cannot change, and to make decisions accordingly.

Step Two, ''Came to believe that a Power greater
than ourselves could restore us to sanity,'' and Step
Three, ''Made a decision to turn our will and our lives
over to the care of God *as we understood Him*,'' com-
bat the isolation we feel and the belief that we alone
have to solve our problems. In working these Steps, we
come to understand that we have an external source of
help. Being aware that we are not alone allows us to
''let go and let God.'' This means stopping the controlling behaviors that have been inherent for so long in
our relationships with others, and recognizing that we
do not have the sole responsibility of solving everyone's problems. For the partner of a man who is addicted to affairs, letting go can include letting go of
control, of anger, and possibly even of the man.

Coaddicts usually have a long history of trying to
control the sex addict's behavior. We throw out the
pornography. At parties we scrutinize his expressions
as he looks at other women and watch him across the

room to see who he's talking with. We don't dare leave town or even leave him alone for the evening. We phone him at work to check on whether he's really there, go through his pockets looking for strange ticket stubs, and inspect his shirts for lipstick stains.

Even after we get into a Twelve Step program and realize we cannot control his behavior—that the addict will always find ways to elude our control—it is hard for us to change our patterns of behavior. First of all, we are used to the behaviors, and we're comfortable with them—they're almost automatic. Second, they served a function in the past. Facing the unmanageability in our lives would have overwhelmed us; thus, our attempts at control helped keep that reality at bay. We had the illusion that we did have some power over his behavior. We had *something to do,* and action is a strong antidote to despair and hopelessness. If we could lose weight, get our hair done, look extra sexy, or buy a new dress, perhaps he would stop being interested in other women. To give up these attempts at control, to face our powerlessness head-on, is frightening, yet it is a necessary first step in the recovery process. The only way to deal with this fear is to replace it with something positive—a belief that our Higher Power is watching out for us so that it is safe to let go.

Steps Two and Three allow us to do Step One without feeling total despair. We can stop trying to do it on our own, because we are not alone. The program does not require acceptance of a traditional God; all it requires is the belief that there is a source of power greater than ourselves. If we are religious, our Higher Power may be God; if we are not, it may be the strength and support of a Twelve Step group, or else the inner resources we were unable to utilize until we found the program. No matter how we define our Higher Power, its presence in our lives means that we are not alone.

Many of us have a great deal of anger and resentment toward our spouse, often so much that there is little hope of saving the marriage. Those of us with a viable marriage have to learn to let go of our anger and resentment—a difficult undertaking. Certain dates, songs, places, people, comments, newspaper articles, and situations will bring back the pain of the past. Suppressing these feelings or saying nothing about them will not keep them away. It is healthier to let our spouse know we are reliving the pain and anger. With time, the intensity of these feelings diminishes and the intervals between episodes of pain and anger lengthen.

If we believe in a Higher Power, we do not take it upon ourselves to punish our spouse for his past misdeeds; we will gradually learn that things somehow work out for the best without our direct intervention, and we trust that we will be shown the way to deal with negative feelings.

An important antidote to anger is realizing how we got into the relationship in the first place. One woman said this about her relationship with a sex addict:

> *I was a volunteer, not a victim. It was no accident that I found myself in a situation which caused me so much pain. I was looking for this kind of person, and I found him. If it hadn't been this particular husband, it would have been another man doing similar things. Knowing this doesn't give me any less reason to be*

angry at the very real hurts I experienced, but it does remind me that I share in the responsibility of having been in that situation.

We can help ourselves by doing a written account of our past experiences with relationships.

• Were your previous romantic partners as loving and as nurturing as you thought you wanted?
• Were they similar to your spouse in their lack of concern for your feelings?
• Were *you* the one who was usually the giver, the accommodating one, the nurturing one?
• Did you feel you did not really deserve any better?
• Did you have any signs before you were married that your husband would not be the ideal mate that you were hoping for?

Many coaddicts who have searched their souls discovered aspects of their own personalities they hadn't seen before, helping them view their role in the relationship in a different light. One young woman related:

I saw myself as a victim my whole life. Men were to fix me and heal me and validate my existence. When people didn't meet my expectations I got very angry. Now I realize that I'm responsible for myself.

Another young woman married to a promiscuous husband said:

I've gathered people around me who have problems to prove that I'm okay. My script has been that

I'm a good person and that I'm a survivor—look at how I get through these terrible situations! I've always lived in crisis—that is the way I define myself. Everyone tells me how wonderful I am, how strong and how helpful. If I didn't have these crises, I wouldn't know who I am. I thought it was an accident that I kept experiencing crises, but now I see that I was using people; I've done it since childhood.

By looking at our past, we can acquire a new understanding of our own behavior; our insights are the first stage of making changes in our lives.

The "letting go" that accompanies Steps Two and Three may involve letting go of another person. As coaddicts, we have been willing to subordinate our own needs to those of the other person. Often, we might have agreed to sexual activities we were uncomfortable with in order to hold on to the other person. In doing this, we let ourselves be treated disrespectfully, perhaps because we did not believe we were really worthy of respect. As part of our recovery process, we learn to treat ourselves with increasing respect and to ask the same treatment from our spouses. We need to set boundaries of what behaviors are acceptable to us and what aren't. If our spouse is not in a Twelve Step program and does not believe that his behavior is problematic, we may need to choose between continuing to live with the unacceptable behaviors or letting go of the other person. Because a sexual relationship is so personal, it is difficult to continue living with someone who has affairs with other women or men. If as sexual coaddicts we subscribe to the belief that sex is the most important sign of love, we're likely to be devastated by his continuing involvement with others. Recovery for us may involve removing ourselves from the situation. Letting go of a person we have been addicted to is very difficult but may be necessary for our recovery.

Steps Four and Five direct us to look at our shortcomings and strengths and to admit them to ourselves, to our Higher Power, and to another human being. Step Four asks us to make a "searching and fearless moral inventory." This may be our first honest look at our strengths and weaknesses in many years. We may have avoided the truth and our feelings for so long that facing the truth and these feelings is frightening. Knowing oneself, however, is necessary in order to be able to make changes.

As we take Step Four we're likely to discover that we are angry and resentful. Up to now we may have been able to justify these feelings—after all, our husband's behavior was certainly deserving of anger and resentment! But when we take a searching look at ourselves, we will find that with time we have become angry and resentful people. Anyone can be angry or resentful at times, but when we are chronically angry and resentful we are unhappy and unhealthy people who are usually depressed, have physical symptoms, or may be engaged in various compulsive behaviors. Recognizing our chronic anger and resentfulness is one of the first steps to making changes.

Codependent people might believe that if other people knew what they were really like, these people would not respect them. According to Step Five, "We admitted to God, to ourselves, and to another person the exact nature of our wrongs.'' Finding a trustworthy person with whom to take Step Five may be the first time we have dared to let someone else know what we are really like. Getting acceptance from this other person no matter what character defects we have revealed (jealousy, insecurity, anger, resentment, emotional withdrawal, criticalness) will assist us in recognizing that we are worthwhile people.

In the following four Steps, we enlist God's help in removing our character defects and then take some concrete actions. In Step Six, we ''Were entirely ready to have God remove all these defects of character,'' and then in Step Seven ''Humbly asked Him to remove our shortcomings.'' In Step Eight, we ''Made a list of all persons we had harmed, and became willing to make amends to them all.'' Finally Step Nine tells us to make ''direct amends to such people wherever possible, except when to do so would injure them or others.'' Our list must include ourselves, for there is no way we can make peace with others unless we can also make peace with ourselves.

Making amends first requires facing the truth about the effects of our behavior on other people. Did our critical attitude cause those around us to feel defensive? Did our need to control cause resentment by those we tried to control? Did our irresponsibility make others have to do our work for us? Did we hurt another woman by our unjustified jealousy? Did we bore our friends with our endless complaints about our husbands and then anger them by our refusal to do anything about our situation after asking their advice?

''Making amends'' to others is painful; it takes courage and humility. But the result is an increased sense of self-worth and peace of mind. The objective of making amends is to accept personal responsibility for our past behavior. This contributes to our self-respect. Amends can consist of a direct apology or other sincere actions made directly to the people harmed, or it may be an indirect reparation such as volunteer work or a financial contribution to a worthy cause.

Steps Ten and Eleven are "maintenance" Steps, designed to help the recovering person live a healthy life. Step Ten states, "Continued to take personal inventory and when we were wrong promptly admitted it." This Step is crucial so the coaddict can monitor the process of her recovery. In addiction to alcohol, recovery and relapse are clear-cut—a recovering alcoholic is one who does not drink; a relapse is resumption of drinking. Recovery and relapse in sex addiction can also be defined in terms of specific behaviors. But codependency consists of so many behaviors that defining recovery and relapse becomes more difficult. To make things even harder, the same behavior may be either healthy or evidence of a relapse or slip, depending on the goal of the behavior. For example, if our husband asks us to go with him to a party and we agree because we think we'll enjoy ourselves, that's healthy. But if we agree because we know that an old flame of his will be there and we believe that our presence will prevent him from spending a lot of time with her—this is an example of the old coaddict type of thinking. In recovery, we must be very honest with ourselves about the motives for our behavior. By monitoring our feelings and thoughts, we can then choose different behaviors.

Two years into recovery, Alice found it increasingly easier to monitor her internal monologue and correct its misconceptions. She told this story at a recovery group meeting.

One day as my husband and I were on our way to a movie, I mentioned something about our twenty-fifth wedding anniversary, which is twenty-one years away. He said, "Maybe we won't be together by then." Instantly my coaddict stomach flipped over, and I thought, He's planning to leave me! *But in the next breath I said to myself, wait a minute! Maybe he's afraid that I'm going to leave him. So I answered him, casually—at least I hoped it sounded casual—"Why, are you afraid I'm going to leave you?" He answered, "Well, yes, I do worry about it sometimes; after all, I've treated you pretty badly at times." What a lesson to me! I had rethought my first reaction, and the revised version had turned out to be correct. Meanwhile, instead of acting like a dependent, fearful wife, I had behaved as though I were self-assured and concerned about his insecurity.*

I am learning that although I cannot control my initial reaction, I can choose what to do subsequently. I can evaluate that first negative reaction, and if it doesn't conform to reality, I can say something positive to myself instead. I can then behave as though I believe it. Each experience like this one decreases the gap between how I behave and what I believe about myself.

We keep our bad feelings going with a constant stream of negative self-talk. If he's late, we think: I wonder if he's stopped off at the bar or a woman friend's house. I'm sure it's my fault. What did I do or say this morning that got him angry? Maybe if I hadn't complained about what he did yesterday, he'd be home by now. Why can't I stop being such a nag? The negative internal monologue is part of our codependency. In recovery, we learn to become aware of the self-defeating talk, to substitute positive self-talk and to behave *as if*. The more we do it, the easier it gets.

Step Eleven, another maintenance Step, states, "Sought through prayer and meditation to improve our conscious contact with God *as we understood Him*, praying only for knowledge of His will for us and the power to carry that out." Daily meditation is a very helpful part of recovery from coaddiction. One way to do this is to each day read and think about a page from the book *One Day at a Time in Al-Anon*. This little book contains brief, thoughtful comments on subjects of concern to recovering codependents such as acceptance, changing what we can, controlling, detachment, honesty with oneself, problem solving, resentment, self-deception, and serenity. Daily recitation of the Serenity Prayer reminds us how to live our lives according to the Twelve Steps: "God, grant me the serenity to accept the things I cannot change, courage to change the things I can, and wisdom to know the difference." This brief prayer essentially summarizes the philosophy of Twelve Step programs.

Finally, the last Step urges us to carry the message of recovery to other people in need and to live our own lives according to the principles of the Steps. Long ago, the founders of A.A. learned that the best way to remain sober was to work with other alcoholics. Seeing the despair and degradation practicing alcoholics experience is a sober reminder to recovering people of what life used to be like and how it could be again if they relapse. Twelfth Step work—that is, talking with the practicing addict or codependent about our own experiences and how we got better—is an integral part of the program.

When, in my medical practice, I advise a patient to go to A.A. or Al-Anon meetings, I often hear, ''But I've heard that those programs are religious—they're always talking about God. I don't believe in God, and I know that I'd be very uncomfortable at those meetings.'' The belief that the Twelve Step program is religious is a misconception. It is not religious, but *spiritual*. It does not require a belief in God, but only a renunciation of our isolation and of the premise that we each are at the center of our own universe. The spiritual program requires an acceptance of the existence of strength and help from sources other than our own intellect. For the atheist or agnostic, the source may be the self-help group, with its support and collective strength. A belief in God is not a requirement for membership in the Twelve Step programs, nor is it necessary for recovery from addiction, even though recovery is very difficult without a willingness to develop one's spirituality.

COMMUNICATING WITH LOVE

Veronica Ray

*Communication is the greatest single factor
affecting a person's health and relationship to others.*
—VIRGINIA SATIR

I've called this article *Communicating with Love* because love is what motivates and enables us to communicate fully, honestly, and sanely. I'm not just talking about communicating with our "loved ones," but about communication based on love for ourselves, our Higher Power, and all other people.

Dr. Gerald Jampolsky writes, "When communication is based on love, it is deeply satisfying and healing." When communication is *not* based on love, it is often based on fear, mistrust, and judgments. These delusions of self-protection hide shame and low self-worth. This kind of communication often results in self-defeating patterns and builds walls between ourselves and others.

On the other hand, communication based on love can revive our relationships and promote our recovery. It can help to free us of our old self-defeating

Reprinted, with changes, with permission of Hazelden Foundation. From *Communicating with Love*, by Veronica Ray. Copyright © 1989 by Hazelden Foundation.

habits. It can help us begin breaking down the walls between ourselves and others. It can change everything.

HOW DO WE COMMUNICATE?

I've always been fascinated by the ability of Mr. Spock (of "Star Trek" fame) to "mind-meld." He places his hand on someone's head, and within seconds that person's knowledge, thoughts, and feelings enter his own mind. He understands the other person's point of view perfectly, without giving up his own.

But we humans are stuck with a much less direct method of communication: talking, listening, observing facial expressions, hand gestures, and other body movements. This process can be complicated and open to a great deal of unclear expression and misinterpretation. Our individual differences can make understanding each other difficult.

While communication may not be easy for most people, the issues of codependency can create special communication problems. In living with another's addiction or compulsion, we may have adapted to lies, mixed messages, suppression, and manipulative, controlling communication.

In recovering from issues of codependency, we may uncover specific communication difficulties. In *Codependent No More*, Melody Beattie observes: "We carefully choose our words to manipulate, people please, control, cover up, and alleviate guilt. Our communication reeks of repressed feelings, repressed thoughts, ulterior motives, low self-worth, and shame. . . . We don't say what we mean; we don't mean what we say."

Often, we don't even know what we mean or want to say. Our patterns of repression, denial, and self-protection may be so deeply ingrained that we've lost touch with our true thoughts and feelings. And when we do know what we are thinking or feeling, we may feel compelled to express it in an indirect way.

Valerie got a phone call early one morning from her sister-in-law, Jenny. Here is their conversation:

Jenny: You have a sewing machine, don't you, Valerie?

Valerie: Yes.

Jenny: Do you use it?

Valerie: Sometimes.

Jenny: Are you going to be home today around four-thirty?

Valerie: Yes.

Jenny: Would that be a good time for Mark to pick up the sewing machine? He'll pass through your neighborhood on his way home from work.

Valerie: Well . . . I guess so.

Jenny: Thanks. I'm going to make some clothes for our trip to California.

Jenny never asked if she could borrow the sewing machine. She manipulated Valerie into lending it to her. From Jenny's point of view, she was just getting what she wanted. It never occurred to her to ask Valerie directly.

Communication Rules

All relationships and systems have communication rules. Some of these rules can be helpful in promoting good communication. Some rules might include:

- not being rude or critical of other people
- respecting other people's privacy
- keeping other people's confidences

Dysfunctional families with codependent relationships may have another set of unwritten rules for communication. These rules are different from those just mentioned because they are often impossible to obey (*always act happy*), hidden (*you should know better than to talk about that with your father*), unfair (*parents can say hurtful things to children, but children must speak with respect to their elders*), out of date (*I don't care how old you are; you're still my child, and you have to do as I say*), or otherwise inappropriate.

Rules in dysfunctional families often have to do with keeping secrets. This is different from respecting confidences because the things we keep secret are our thoughts, feelings, and experiences in family life. The "don't talk, don't trust, don't feel" rule, common to many families where addictions, compulsions, or physical or sexual abuse are present, may have taught us to lock our thoughts and feelings deep inside.

Inappropriate rules often involve taboos. In some families, it may be unthinkable to disagree with other family members or to be uninvolved in every aspect of each other's life. In some relationships, certain feelings, topics, or ways of expressing (such as hugging, questioning, or arguing) are forbidden, even if no one ever says so.

Later in life, these kinds of rules can create difficulty in knowing what our feelings are, being able to talk about them, and being able to trust people enough to talk to them. We may feel compelled to offer advice or opinions on matters that are not our business. We may find ourselves habitually lying or repressing our true feelings. We may say anything we think will gain other people's approval.

Unable to express ourselves clearly, we may feel perpetually misunderstood. We may have a great deal of difficulty allowing anyone to get close to us. The old rules can sabotage our current relationships, creating confusion, unhappiness, and even physical pains and illnesses.

Breaking the Roles and Rules

In recovering from the issues of codependency, we may begin to uncover our hidden feelings. We can begin understanding the systems in which we've lived and our roles in them. We can recognize the old communication rules and start breaking them. We can make up new rules to better serve our current needs.

Again, let's remember not to fall into blaming others or shaming ourselves for our old roles and rules. We have done our best to survive this far. Now we can examine our survival strategies and assess the cost to our health, happiness, and well-being.

We can stop paying the price of confused, restricted, and unsatisfying communication. We can learn to identify our real thoughts and feelings, and learn to express them clearly and respectfully. We can open our minds and hearts to a deeper understanding of others. We may not be able to "mind-meld," but we can improve our relationships and our lives through improved communication.

IDENTIFYING AND ACCEPTING OUR THOUGHTS AND FEELINGS

Communication with the self always comes first. We can't be honest with others if we aren't honest with ourselves.

—AMY E. DEAN

For many of us working through codependency issues, the hardest part of communication is knowing what we want to communicate. When we are with other people, our own thoughts and feelings may fly right out of our heads. We may instantly begin caretaking, people pleasing, approval seeking, or trying to manage other people's impressions of us in other ways.

As we try to find the true self behind our outer shield, we may feel a great deal of resistance. We may feel more comfortable with familiar behavior, even when we know it's hurting us. We may believe deeply that our old ways still protect us somehow. We may be afraid to unleash our deepest inner thoughts and feelings.

But we can overcome all of this resistance. Facing our thoughts and feelings doesn't make them any more real—they're already real. We haven't succeeded in getting rid of them by pretending they weren't there. By facing our fears honestly, we can stop giving them the power to paralyze us.

We can understand our feelings of resistance and accept them. We can gently move forward, one step at a time, through self-awareness and self-acceptance. Our communication with others begins with and depends on our communication with ourselves.

Self-Awareness

In *The Disowned Self,* Nathaniel Branden writes, "Healthy change necessarily begins with self-awareness." If we have been repressing and denying our true thoughts and feelings, it may seem nearly impossible to uncover them again. But we can use our minds, bodies, and other people to help us discover what we really think and how we really feel.

Our inner thoughts and feelings have not gone away, even if we've lost touch with them. They are still within us, and they are sending out signals all the time. Our bodies provide wonderful tools for recognizing what's going on inside us. If there's something hurting on the outside, chances are good there's something hurting on the inside.

Some of us may resist the idea that our aches, pains, and illnesses could be linked to our emotions. We may feel this implies that our physical problems are somehow our fault. This could lead us to insist that our aches, pains, insomnia, depression, and even being accident-prone have purely physical causes.

Letting Go of Self-Blame

Having physical manifestations of repressed or denied emotions doesn't mean we're crazy—it means we're human. We don't have aches, pains, or illnesses because we're bad people. Sometimes those aches, pains, and illnesses carry important messages for us. If our deep inner feelings are trying to get our attention through our bodies, that's a *blessing*. It's a gift through which we can learn, grow, and find true mental, emotional, and physical health.

In other words, physical ailments that our repressed emotions either cause or contribute to are real. Finding an inner message behind the pain doesn't mean the pain doesn't hurt. So let's stop putting ourselves down and open up to the wisdom our bodies can share with us.

Wanda's Story

"When I was growing up with two drug-addicted parents and all the family chaos that entails, I got sick a lot," Wanda says. "I always had headaches and stomachaches. The doctor couldn't find anything wrong with me, and said it was 'just nerves.' "

As an adult, Wanda continued having physical problems but rarely saw a doctor. "I was always afraid they'd say it was 'just nerves' again," she explains. "I didn't want to be seen as a hypochondriac."

After a failed marriage to a chemically dependent man, Wanda began working through her codependency and Adult Child issues. "I learned how much old pain, fear, and anger I had stuffed away over the years. But it had all come out—in my body. The more I worked through all the old feelings, the better I felt. I learned to accept all my inner experiences as a valid part of me. I didn't like everything I found there, but I accepted it and began loving myself anyway.''

Of course, all aches, pains, and illnesses cannot be quickly or easily alleviated by discovering our hidden thoughts and feelings. Our mission here is not to cure the body but to learn to hear what it can teach us. Wanda learned to respect her body's ability to reflect her inner experience. She released some old buried thoughts and emotions and started taking better care of herself. All of this together allowed her to enjoy better health.

Knowing Oneself Means Observing Oneself and Talking with Others

By observing our actions, we can uncover many of the thoughts and feelings we've forbidden ourselves to talk about. For example, acting superior to others is often an indication of low self-esteem. Vanity can mask deep feelings of inadequacy and an inability to accept one's appearance. Depression can indicate anger turned inward. Paranoia can cover up guilt, shame, and self-hatred. In John Powell's book, *Why Am I Afraid to Tell You Who I Am?*, he says, ''Exaggerated behavior in a person usually means just the opposite of what it implies.''

Other people can also help us find our buried thoughts and feelings. We can talk with counselors, therapists, or others who can help us see ourselves more clearly. Even saying, ''I don't know how I feel'' can elicit helpful feedback in the form of descriptions about how we look, speak, act, and behave. The way we really feel is hidden in there somewhere, and other people can often help us find it.

Gaining self-awareness isn't as difficult as we may believe. Everything is right here, within each of us, waiting to be found. Only our fears keep us blocked from exploring our own inner experience. With trust and faith in our Higher Power, we can accept our fears and move on in spite of them. We can discover that what we learn about ourselves won't hurt us, but keeping it locked away deep inside already has.

Self-Acceptance

Once we have uncovered a personal belief or feeling, we can accept it. This doesn't mean we necessarily approve of it or resign ourselves to having it forever. It also doesn't mean we have to act on our feeling. It simply means that we claim ownership of it. We recognize and admit that it is a part of us right now.

In her book, *Holding Back: Why We Hide the Truth about Ourselves,* Marie Lindquist writes, "Self-acceptance means accepting yourself as a work-in-progress. It means believing that you are okay in spite of your flaws and believing that you have the strength and the power to change."

If we think of ourselves as "works-in-progress," anything is possible. We can discover where we are right now and what we need to work on. We can let go of old shame, ask for help from our Higher Power and other people, and begin moving in the direction we want to go.

Accepting our inner beliefs, thoughts, and feelings is necessary for learning to communicate. Until we accept ourselves as we are, we can't express ourselves honestly or change whatever needs to be changed.

Betty's Dilemma and How She Solved It

Betty and Gina became friends in school and kept in touch for many years. They only saw each other once or twice a year. Every time they did get together, Betty would suffer a terrible headache afterward. "It seemed like I was allergic to Gina," Betty laughs. "But I now know the real reason for my headaches: all the time I've known Gina, I've been jealous of her. I never admitted it, even to myself, but it's true. I could never be happy for her successes, although I tried to act like I was. I hated myself for being so jealous. Gina had always been a good friend. What it came down to was, I just didn't like myself. It really had nothing to do with Gina personally."

Betty faced up to her low self-esteem and accepted it as a part of her, even though it was a part she didn't like. "I didn't want to accept it for a long time. I always thought of acceptance as giving up, resigning myself to being that way forever. But once I did accept it as something inside me *right then,* I could start working toward a future time when it would no longer be a part of me. Working on my self-image, self-respect, and self-love has produced better results than years of trying to work on my relationship with Gina."

We can start improving our communication with others by learning what we want to communicate and what we're already communicating (even if we don't realize it). We begin by accepting ourselves honestly so we can communicate honestly to others. With the help of our Higher Power and other people, we can learn to communicate with ourselves openly, honestly, and lovingly.

Meditation Exercise

Relax, close your eyes, and ask yourself: *How do I feel right now?*

- If your feeling were a color, what color would it be? A bright, vibrant color? A dark one? Or a soft pastel?
- If your feeling were an animal, what animal would it be? A ferocious wild animal? A cool, sleek sea animal? Or a domestic pet?
- If your feeling were a shape, what shape would it be? A sharp, angular shape? Or a soft, rounded one?
- If your feeling were a sound, what sound would it be? A loud, blasting, melodious, shrill, deep, or cooing sound?
- Are you on a beach, a mountaintop, a busy city street, or in a cool, dark cave?
- Now think about the underlying feeling of such choices as a fox or an owl, bright red or pale pink, ice cream or hot coffee, a blizzard or a thunderstorm, running water or an alarm, a waterfall or a concrete parking lot.
- What feelings do they make you think of?
- What feelings could be hiding inside you?
- Just accept whatever you find without making judgments.

EXPRESSING OURSELVES

Self-disclosure is a social skill, not a mysterious rite. Like all social skills, it can be learned, practiced, and improved upon.

—MARIE LINDQUIST

Once we've learned to recognize and own our thoughts and feelings, the next step is communicating them to others. We have many tools for accomplishing this: written words, spoken words and other sounds, our tone of voice, facial expressions, hand gestures, posture, and other body movements.

We also express ourselves in more subtle ways. Where we sit in a room with other people can show how we feel about them and about being there. The physical distance we keep between ourselves and others when we're talking with them can reveal our feelings. Choosing whether to stand or sit can establish our communication role.

All of our expressions—overt and subtle, deliberate and unconscious—combine to form the messages we send to others. When the various parts of our expression disagree with each other, misunderstandings often result. "Nothing is wrong" may come out of our mouths while we slam doors, stomp around, and make tight, angry faces. Such double messages can promote mistrust, since we clearly aren't being honest.

To avoid such blocked communication, we can learn to say what we really mean. We can examine all our verbal and nonverbal messages and learn to express ourselves openly, honestly, and clearly.

Asking Ourselves, *What Is My Goal?*

Before attempting any communication, we can define our goal or purpose. If we're honest with ourselves, we can avoid many misunderstandings and confrontations simply by considering this question.

For example, if your purpose is to hurt someone's feelings—because the person has hurt you, or for any other reason—the message is not worth sending. If honest examination reveals that your true purpose is to control another person, don't do it. Let it go. Respecting other people's rights and self-esteem is an important part of good communication.

This doesn't mean we can never say anything another person might not want to hear. If what we have to say can help our relationship, or if we need to say it to take care of ourselves, we can say it—*respectfully*.

Respecting others also doesn't mean we can never ask someone for a favor or something else that we want. It means we do it honestly and clearly, in a straightforward manner. We don't lie, manipulate, bully, or shame others into doing what we want. And if we don't get what we want, we can accept it graciously and figure out what we need to do next to take care of ourselves.

Our communication goal or purpose may be solving a problem or strengthening a relationship. It may be taking care of ourselves by saying no. Our purpose might be sharing facts. Or it could be resolving a conflict or just enjoying someone's company. Whatever the goal is, keeping our true goal in mind can help us communicate more effectively. It can help us avoid being sidetracked into old roles and rules. It can help us stay focused on *expression* rather than *impression*. Trying to manage another's impression of us is not healthy communication—it's dishonesty and manipulation. And it's usually not very effective. Clear expression is the surest way to let other people know who we are.

Words

Words are the most obvious part of our expression. They are also probably the easiest to change with a little conscious effort. To improve our verbal communication, we don't have to learn new words. It's how we *use* words that makes the difference.

Up to now, our word choices may have been primarily based on old roles, rules, and habits. Now we can become aware of our choices and how they affect others. We can learn to use words clearly and honestly, and avoid negative and hurtful words. We can improve our relationships and our own well-being through the responsible use of language.

Since no two people can experience the world in exactly the same way, people often have different definitions and connotations for many words and phrases. Some words that don't bother you at all may trigger negative reactions in others. In a relationship, it is worth noticing and respecting your partner's trigger words.

Sandy's Trigger Word

Sandy is the mother of four children between the ages of two and fourteen. She hasn't held a job outside of homemaking and motherhood since the birth of her

first child. "I see red when people say I 'don't work,' "
she says. "It makes me especially mad to hear my
husband say it. He knows how hard I work raising our
children, cleaning, cooking, shopping, growing vege-
tables, running errands. It's what I choose to do, and I
love it. But it really drives me crazy when people don't
want to call it *work!*"

The people who say Sandy "doesn't work" probably
don't mean to disrespect her. They simply mean she
doesn't hold a job outside the home. But *work* is clearly
a trigger word for Sandy.

Common Trigger Words

Some words seem to be triggers for most, if not all,
of us. For example, *you, should, always,* and *never*
often cause communication problems. Beginning a sentence with *you* can make it sound like an attack. The
usual response to an attack is defense (which is really a
counterattack). Attack/defend communication isn't
open, honest, productive, or conducive to happy relationships. But if we make our point without judgments,
the other person is free to respond to what we've said
rather than to being attacked.

Words like *always* and *never* are inflexible and rarely
appropriate. They make it difficult to stay focused on
the present. The word *should* implies a personal judgment. Any word that labels or judges people can have
harmful effects on our attempts to communicate.

Words to Communicate Clearly and Respectfully

Choosing positive, respectful words, and taking responsibility for ourselves by using "I," can turn angry

or confused exchanges into good communication.

Let's look at some examples:

- Instead of attacking, "You should never have taken that last turn," you could suggest, "I think if we go back to that last turn, we can find our way."
- Rather than complaining, "You should have been here an hour ago," you could state, "I expected you an hour ago."
- Instead of declaring, "You never call when you say you will," you could explain, "I expected you to call today. I felt hurt when you didn't."

Using metaphors and analogies can sometimes help us communicate more clearly. For example, if a doctor is explaining the working of a hip or shoulder joint to a young patient, he or she may talk about ball bearings. In literature about addictions and codependency, we often talk about emotional "merry-go-rounds" or "roller coasters."

Humor can be another useful tool in communication. But it must be handled with care. It isn't funny to put down another person's feelings or point of view. It isn't funny to ridicule or humiliate others. Humor used negatively can hurt instead of help. On the other hand, humor used positively can diffuse tension and bring people together. Positive humor respects everyone's self-esteem, is appropriate to the time and place, and is not distracting.

Honesty, like humor, requires some care. In some cases, replying "That's none of your business" is more appropriate than either lying to protect your privacy or revealing more than you feel comfortable with. Again, we must remember to respect *everyone's* self-esteem. If we hate someone's new haircut, we don't have to say so. And we don't have to go overboard saying we love it. We can ask how that person likes it. We can say it looks cool for the summer heat or easy to take care of. We can be truthful without attacking another's self-esteem.

Being Honest and Direct
About What We Want and Don't Want

We may think we're asking for what we want when we're actually attacking someone for not having given it to us already. Instead of screaming, "Why don't you ever help me around here?" you can say, "I need help with this." Rather than whining, "Why do we always have to do whatever you want to do?" you can say, "I want to go to the movies tonight."

Making up excuses for things we don't want to do is a confused, dishonest way of saying *no*. We may not have believed it in the past, but we do have the right to refuse requests, invitations, and other people's attempts to manipulate us. For example, rather than sighing, "Can't you get someone else to do it?" you can simply say, "No." Instead of stammering, "Well, gee . . . I don't know . . . I might have to do something else that night," you can simply say, "No, but thank you for asking me."

Outright lying is not part of loving communication. We may have done it in the past because of shame, fear, or mistrust, and it may have become a habit. Letting go of habitual lying can improve our communication with others dramatically. We can practice just keeping quiet instead of lying. When we realize that our silence holds no danger, we can take the next step and begin to replace our lies with truthfulness. The protection we thought lying provided can then be replaced by real trust and respect in our relationships.

How Letter Writing Can Help

The only time we express ourselves solely through words is in writing. Writing can help us clarify our thoughts and choose our words before talking with people. It can also replace face-to-face discussion in the form of a letter.

First, forget what you were taught in school about things like headings, greetings, and spelling. Anyone who can put words on paper can write a letter. Just remember your goal—expression, not impression.

Letter writing gives us the chance to change our minds as we go along. Sometimes, in speech, words slip out before we realize it. In writing, we can edit in order to say what we want to say and leave out the rest. So take advantage of this by taking the time to rewrite.

All of the things we've already said about positive words, using ''I,'' avoiding attack/defend, and using metaphors apply to letter writing. And remember, you don't have to write ten pages unless you want to. A simple note saying, ''I've been thinking about you,'' or ''I'm sorry,'' or ''Thank you'' can mean more than page after page of eloquent prose. Once you've said what you have to say, stop.

Words are powerful tools for communication. Handled with a little care, they can express our true thoughts and feelings and improve our relationships. And that can change our lives.

Body Language

Leo Buscaglia writes, "Where words fail, it is comforting to realize how many other vital and eloquent ways we have of communicating with each other." Sometimes just a touch, smile, or nod says everything. Sometimes just looking straight at someone instead of looking away says, *I'm listening and I care.*

Even while we're talking, our bodies constantly send out messages. Nonverbal communication is produced by the combination of our vocal tone and pitch, hand gestures, eye and facial movements, the tilt of our heads, and the position of our entire bodies.

It is important to understand body language because it's happening whether we know it or not. If we're unaware of what our bodies say, we miss the opportunity to express ourselves fully. If our body sends a different message than our words, people are likely to misunderstand or mistrust us. But when our verbal and nonverbal messages agree, communication can be clear and honest.

First we can learn what our body movements are, and what they say to others. Do you know how you look right now? Your facial expression, posture, head movement, hand gestures? What does your voice sound like? Are you physically relaxed, tense, graceful, stiff, slow, quick, or nervous?

How Will Found Out About His Body Language

"I once had the unnerving experience of being seated directly opposite a mirrored wall in a restaurant," Will says. "All evening, I could see myself talking, laughing, frowning, smiling, looking interested, looking bored, and looking very uncomfortable. Although I smiled and laughed, my discomfort with my host was obvious. While I said nothing, my negative reactions to certain bits of conversation were clearly expressed on my face. I looked away, looked down, covered my mouth with my hand, shook my head, and raised my eyebrows. I leaned forward, leaned back, and crossed my arms in front of me. Every move I made belied what I was secretly thinking and feeling."

Most of us are shocked at first to watch ourselves on a video tape recorder. It's hard to know what our faces and bodies are doing while we're thinking about what we're saying. A video camera can be a great help in this, but it isn't necessary.

Developing Self-Awareness of Body Language

We can start becoming aware of what it feels like to make certain gestures, movements, and facial expressions. We can make a habit of frequently checking to see what our bodies are doing during conversations. We can notice what our bodies feel like, what our faces are doing, where our hands are.

We can also ask others what they saw or heard from us, especially when we feel we've been misunderstood. And we can remember to accept what they tell us, even if it isn't what we felt or intended to express. That's the point—to discover how we come across to others.

The best position for good communication is face-to-face at eye level and within arm's length. This means that if we are talking with a child, we can get down on our knees or have the child sit or stand on something. Likewise, if we want to talk with someone taller, we can ask the other person to sit down, positioning ourselves at eye level with him or her.

It is best to get within arm's length so that we don't have to strain to hear each other. This also helps us focus our attention. We can't feel respected or listened to when the person we're trying to communicate with is facing away from us or doing something else with his or her eyes and ears.

Eye contact is important and often difficult for us. Sometimes we feel intimidated by direct eye contact because we're not used to such undivided attention. Sometimes we avert our eyes due to shyness, self-consciousness, or shame. Sometimes we avoid eye contact because we're lying. In any case, we can become aware of our behaviors and change them. Direct eye contact is an excellent way to improve non-verbal communication. It helps people trust us and feel more connected to us when we're talking with them.

Body language isn't difficult to understand. All it takes is an awareness of our physical positions and movements.

- How do they feel?
- What do they look like?
- What are they saying to others?
- Are they expressing the same thoughts and feelings as your words?
- Is your face tight or relaxed?
- Are your arms folded or hanging at your sides?
- Are your hands waving, pointing, or in your pockets?
- Is your voice tight, dry, squeaky, loud, or hoarse?
- Do you feel like steel or jelly? A mountain or a pebble? A flowing stream or an erupting volcano?

Understanding the verbal and nonverbal messages we send out can help us communicate more effectively. We can think of ourselves as television stations, sending out sounds and pictures. Both are important for our audience to understand us. We can develop them as separate skills. Then, together, they can blend into accurate, honest, clear communication.

Practicing Self-Disclosure

We learn to express ourselves more honestly and clearly in order to let others know who we are. If we are not used to letting others know us, we'll face many new questions. Just as verbal and nonverbal expression takes practice, so does choosing the times, places, and people with whom to use it.

Our therapists, counselors, and Twelve Step groups are good people with whom to start practicing open, honest, direct communication. We can practice using clear, positive words and harmonious body language.

We can try out new behaviors without fear. When we know our listeners support us, we can often express ourselves more clearly.

With time and practice, we can use our new tools of expression with an ever-widening circle of people. We can discover the joy of open, honest, and loving communication in all of our relationships.

Exercises on Self-Expression

Exercise One

When you find yourself in a difficult conversation, take a short break to clear your mind. Excuse yourself and go someplace where you can get away by yourself for a moment. Close your eyes, relax, and take a couple of deep breaths.

- Now ask yourself: *What is my goal?* Keep your true goal in mind as you return to the conversation, saying what you think and feel, calmly and clearly, and listening to the other person's point of view.
- Or, if you need more time to sort out your thoughts and feelings, ask the other person(s) to finish the discussion later, and then agree on a specific time to meet again.

Exercise Two

Make a list of your "trigger" words.

- Let the people who are important to you know what these words are.
- Make an effort to avoid other people's trigger words when you are communicating with them.

LISTENING WITH LOVE

I believe the very best in us is brought out when we truly listen to others, because to do so requires some of the noblest of human traits.

—LEO BUSCAGLIA

Most of us probably think we're pretty good at listening. After all, we do it all the time with almost no effort. But listening in a way that helps good communication—listening with love—means more than just hearing words.

I once took a course taught by a woman with terminal cancer. She was blind in one eye and deaf in one ear. She wore a hearing aid in the other ear and a prosthesis in her mouth. And yet, with all of these handicaps, she was able to communicate with the class fully and enthusiastically. Awestruck by this woman, I felt blessed to be in the last class she ever taught.

Besides the courageous inspiration this teacher provided, there was another reason I got more out of her class than any other. I had to *listen* harder. My eyes never left her when she was speaking or reacting to something someone else said. The usual chatter in my mind hushed as I concentrated on understanding her.

Without knowing it at the time, I was practicing all the requirements of listening with love. I gave my full, undivided attention. I wasn't thinking about what I wanted to say, or my next class, or the lovely spring weather outside. I didn't assume that I knew what the teacher was going to say, or that I could pick up the gist of it without much effort. I asked questions and let her know whether or not I had understood her.

Seeing and Hearing

Essentially, listening is paying attention to someone. The first thing we have to do in order to truly listen is eliminate distractions. As M. Scott Peck wrote in his book, *The Road Less Traveled,* "The act of attending requires that we make the effort to set aside our existing preoccupations . . . and actively shift our consciousness."

Eliminating Distractions

When Brian's alcoholic brother, Jack, was hospitalized, Brian and his wife made the four-hour drive to see him. "After visiting Jack in the hospital, we went to my parents' house," Brian recalls. "We had to drive back home that evening, but we wanted to talk about Jack's condition and what had been happening in the family.

"We sat down and tried to talk, but there was a football game on TV. It was loud and distracting, but no one turned it off or even lowered the volume. It was pretty hard to have a serious conversation with a TV blaring in the room. After about fifteen minutes, my wife and I gave up and left. My parents had said they were concerned about Jack and wanted to discuss it with me, but their actions had made it impossible."

It *is* difficult to communicate with others over a blaring television. It's more than just simple courtesy to turn off a TV, radio, or stereo when someone is trying to communicate with us. It tells others that we're available to them, that we're willing to set aside our existing preoccupations and pay attention to what they have to say.

Focusing Our Attention

Noise isn't the only distraction we may allow to interfere with good listening. Sometimes we try to listen while doing other things.

Brenda came home from a job interview and tried to tell her husband, James, about it. "I was *so* excited," Brenda remembers. "The interview had been wonderful! I wanted to tell James everything that had happened. But while I talked, he kept doing things—making a sandwich, cleaning up the kitchen, looking at the mail—he even left the room a couple of times! Finally, I stopped talking in midsentence. I felt like a balloon that had been popped. A few minutes later, he came over to me and said, 'So the interview went well, huh?' All I could say was 'Yep,' and I stormed off to take a shower."

James wasn't trying to ignore Brenda. He was actually very happy her interview had gone so well. He just didn't think about her desire to express herself about it and to share with him a happy, exciting experience she'd had. He missed an opportunity to get to know Brenda better, to let her know he cared about her—to *communicate* with her. The making of a sandwich, cleaning the kitchen, and looking at mail all could have waited.

If it's impossible to give someone our attention when he or she wants to talk, we can just say so. Saying "I'm sorry, but I can't listen to you right now. Can we talk at eight o'clock?" would let the person know we're interested in what he or she has to say, but we're just not available at the moment. But before we do that, it's a good idea to ask ourselves if whatever we're doing can wait.

If we're in a bad mood and don't feel like listening to anyone, we can say that, too. Bad moods pass, and we can become available to listen later. That's better than pretending to listen while we're really thinking about ourselves and our problems.

Opening Our Eyes, Ears, Minds, and Hearts

Besides eliminating distractions, we can let go of all our preconceived ideas about what the other person is going to say. Sometimes we let assumptions, expectations, and prejudices tell us what people have to say before they even open their mouths. Often, we're really projecting our own thoughts and feelings onto others.

"I was once sitting in a plane waiting for take-off when several latecomers boarded noisily," Connie says. "I'd just had a wonderfully relaxing vacation, felt great, and hadn't even noticed the few extra minutes we were waiting on the ground for these passengers who'd been delayed in customs. They made such a racket getting aboard, that many of us, who had already settled down with books and magazines, looked up when they came into the cabin. One of the late arrivals, apparently upset by this, shouted to her husband down the aisle, 'Look how they're looking at us, George—as if it's *our fault*!' "

Projection is when we take our own feelings and thoughts and believe they belong to others. Perhaps the woman on the plane felt guilty for the delay—or impatient. In any case, the message was coming from inside her, not from the people who happened to look up when she appeared.

To be free of projection, we can open our minds to whatever people say to us—both verbally and nonverbally. We can let go of our own point of view for a while and respect theirs.

When we listen to another's words, we can remember they might have different definitions or connotations for those words than we do. The best way to make sure we are understanding someone is to ask questions. We can say, "Are you saying . . ." or "Do you mean . . ." and then repeat what we think they have said.

We can also remember that others have old programming that may be affecting their communication with us today. We know how our old tapes can come back to us without warning or be triggered by something outside us. The same is true for other people. We may inadvertently trigger one of their old tapes or get caught in the cross fire when something else does.

The Greek philosopher Diogenes wrote, "We have two ears and only one tongue in order that we may hear more and speak less." I might add to this idea that we also have two eyes. People can tell us as much, if not more, with their bodies as with their words. If we watch for nonverbal messages, we can get a more complete picture of what others are trying to communicate to us.

Empathy

In order to listen fully to others, we need to let go of our own point of view and try to see things from theirs. But we may resist empathizing with others. We may fear that losing sight of our own point of view, even for a moment, will somehow mean losing our selves. We may harbor a deep (even unconscious) belief that everyone's interest is ultimately self-centered, and therefore a person's point of view is necessarily biased to his or her benefit and to our detriment.

But opening ourselves to truly seeing and hearing others can improve all our relationships. It can also promote our individual growth process. As M. Scott Peck wrote, "This unification of speaker and listener is actually an extension and enlargement of ourself, and new knowledge is always gained from this."

Empathy doesn't mean we always have to agree with others. But we can be open to what they have to say and accept it, without personal judgment, as their reality. Improved relationships, expanded knowledge and understanding, and personal growth are all ingredients of increased well-being. Listening with love gives as much to ourselves as it does to others.

RESPONDING WITH LOVE

When we open ourselves to other people, we may receive a variety of communications: blaming and attack, manipulation and control, double messages, or just plain nonsense. We may also receive self-disclosure and love. Let's look at our possible responses to some of these messages.

Blaming and Attack

We have already discussed some of the possible causes underlying blaming and attack. If we remain calm and let the attack go by unanswered, we can respond to the real feeling beneath. With empathy and perhaps humor, we can diffuse the negative tone of such communication.

Manipulation and Control

We can respond to other people's attempts to manipulate and control us in much the same way. We can refuse to respond to the manipulation and try to get at whatever is going on underneath.

For example, if a parent uses guilt to try to make a grown daughter call, write, or visit another relative, the adult daughter can say, "I'm an adult now, and whether I call, write, or visit anyone is my decision. But I still love you and appreciate all you've done for me." The manipulation technique (guilt) has been bypassed, the request answered, and the underlying fear of a parent losing the love of a grown child has been addressed.

We can also point out the controlling behavior. But we'll want to be careful not to judge or attack when we do this. For example, Valerie (who, you may recall, allowed Jenny to manipulate her into borrowing her sewing machine) might have said, "Jenny, you're manipulating me and that's a rotten thing to do." This probably would *not* have improved the tone of their conversation. But, if Valerie had said something like "Jenny, are you asking me if you may borrow my sewing machine?" it would have shifted the communication to a more direct, honest level.

Double Messages

These can be confusing and hard to respond to. If someone's words say something different than his or her body language or behavior, we can ignore one of the messages or express our confusion and ask the person to clarify his or her meaning. For example, if we suggest going to a certain movie and our spouse frowns, but says "Okay," we can take him at his word and go to the movie. Or we can respond to the frown by suggesting a different movie or asking him where he'd like to go. On the other hand, we can say, "I'm confused. You said 'Okay,' but you're frowning. I'm not sure what you're trying to tell me."

Nonsense

Sometimes we may find ourselves faced with communication that is incoherent, irrational, or otherwise distorted by someone's addiction. First, it's usually best to avoid trying to communicate with people when they are under the influence of alcohol or other chemicals. They simply aren't available for communication then.

Second, we can remember Melody Beattie's words, "If it doesn't make sense, it doesn't make sense. We don't have to waste our time trying to make sense of it or trying to convince the other person that what he or she said didn't make sense." Instead, we can accept the reality that the other person isn't making sense, thereby protecting our own sanity.

Honest Self-Disclosure

But not all the messages we receive from others will be negative. When we listen lovingly to others, we may sometimes receive honest self-disclosure from them. If we're not used to it, this can be even more difficult for us to respond to than negative communication.

"Marie and I met in an evening class at a local college," Suzanne explains. "I considered us to be 'acquaintances,' not friends. But I liked her and thought maybe we'd get to be friends in time.

"Then, by coincidence, she moved into a house across the street from mine. She came over for coffee one morning and started telling me about an argument she'd had with her husband. It was nothing serious, just a disagreement. But her talking about it made me very uncomfortable. I kept thinking, *Why is she telling me this? I don't know her well enough to talk about this kind of stuff.*

"I'd wanted to be Marie's friend, but when she opened up to me, I panicked. I was afraid to give an opinion on what she was telling me. And I didn't want to start telling her *my* business the way she was telling me hers. I just wanted to get out of that conversation."

Do We Have to Disclose Ourselves in Return?

When others open up to us, we don't have to judge them or judge what they're saying. We don't have to offer an opinion or a solution to their problem. We don't have to disclose ourselves in return, if we don't want to. The other person may just feel like talking. Or the person may be trying to let us know she trusts us and wants us to know her better.

If people ask for our opinion and we want to give it to them, we can do so—honestly, but kindly. Other times the best way we can help others who want to talk is just by listening and occasionally rephrasing and repeating something they've said. This lets them know we're paying attention to them and can help them clarify their thoughts and feelings.

Accepting Love from Others

While we all want to receive love from others, we don't always know how to accept it. When someone pays us a compliment, do we accept it thankfully, or do we protest that we really don't deserve it? When others say they care about us or understand us, do we believe them?

Our Twelve Step groups can be good places to start accepting self-disclosure and love from others. We can listen lovingly when others tell their stories, and express our understanding without judgments. We can tell our stories and accept the compassion and understanding of our peers. We can learn to listen—and respond—with love.

A Final Note . . .

Even when we work at direct, honest communication, we may not always get the results we want. Communication is a two-way street, and we can only control our side of it.

It is a very human need to be understood and accepted. But we don't need the understanding and acceptance of *everyone*, and trying to get it is futile. Sometimes other people may disagree with us, sometimes we may be wrong, and sometimes others simply won't be able to receive our messages.

We can't force others to see things through our eyes.

They won't always empathize with us, even when we try to empathize with them. In good, healthy, loving communication, we do our best and then let go of the results.

The rewards of communicating with love can be great. Freedom from dishonesty and controlling, manipulative behavior results in better relationships and overall well-being. Good communication can bring us joy and peace. It can be a way to love our Higher Power, other people, and ourselves—and we all deserve that.

POWER PLAYS

Brenda Schaeffer

Love is a fact of life. Not one of us escapes its effects. Love feels good, love feels bad, and the reasons why are anything but simple. In some fashion, our lives center around love, be it self-love, parent-child love, the loss of a love object, or a love relationship that is floundering. When we consider love, we long for a mature, interdependent love that reflects the ultimate goal to which humans can aspire and fills our souls with a sense of spiritual bonding with another. Mature love is an ideal toward which we strive and actually do experience from time to time.

The truth is, most love relationships harbor some elements of addiction. When love becomes obsessive, habitual, or necessary, it often feels bad! Addictive lovers are saying, *If I take care of you and love you the way I want you to love me, then you'll love me that way, too!* Our addictive love for another unconsciously seeks to get our unmet needs fulfilled, to provide us safety and predictability, and to avoid pain. The paradox is this: We fall into addictive love as an attempt to gain control of our lives, and in so doing, we lose control by relinquishing our personal power to another.

Elements of unhealthy dependency creep into the best of love relationships. Most, if not all, relationships give evidence of dependency. Love addiction in itself is not bad. It just is! The hurtful behaviors that accompany it are what we need to rid ourselves of.

Love and addiction are separate entities that may come together for a time, and one can be mistaken for the other. Our challenge is to move from addiction to healthy belonging, no easy task. For as we do, as we begin to give up the predictable and unconsciously agreed upon, we may find ourselves involved in power struggles. At the same time, we want to change and we want to stay the same. And so, we develop another kind of dependency, a competitive one. The telltale signs of it are *power plays*.

Power plays occur whenever there is a threat, real or imagined, to the unhealthy relationship. What was once a complementary agreement between the partners becomes competitive. The battles can be subtle or openly fierce. If power plays are present, we can be sure our love is addictive. And sometimes, playing power games is an addiction in itself!

POWER

Definition: CONTROL—*power* to regulate, direct, or dominate. The word *power* is used in many contexts. In our context—the realm of the quest of love and healthy *inter*dependence in our relationships—the power to strive for is personal potency that springs from self-esteem, not from attempting to gain control over others through power plays.

Most of us are, have been, or want to be in a primary love relationship. We need to love and be loved to bloom to our fullest. We are *interdependent* in a relationship with another if we are able to trust ourselves and our partner, maintaining our individuality even as we are part of the relationship. Mature love affirms the personal power of both lovers. In true love, lovers recognize each other as equals; they are not caught up in mind games and "oneupmanship." When two people are content and free as individuals, they are much more likely to have a content and free love relationship.

Every one of us feels some dependency on our relationship partner, but when we fear we couldn't survive without our relationship and resort to manipulation or control of a lover to get our needs met, we are exhibiting unhealthy signs. Dependent, obsessive love limits our ability to feel content, our capacity for intimacy, and our ability to experience fulfilling love.

One of the most pronounced features of an overly dependent, unhealthy relationship is the use of *power plays* to gain a misguided sense of control over one's partner. Power plays are manipulative or controlling behaviors directed at keeping the relationship partners involved in a "one-up, one-down" melodrama. Not only do they signal an addictive, dependent relationship, but the excitement and drama of these power games are addictive in themselves.

Learning to recognize and withdraw from power plays is a step toward purging them from our relationships and avoiding relationships altogether in which they are likely. We can then be free to love each other as equals.

The myth underlying power plays is that there somehow is not enough power for both people in the relationship, that one person must maintain control over the other. The myth is based on the idea that power is scarce: the people with power believe they have control and can get what they want and need. Without such control, life seems fragile and uncertain. And of course, we all want certainty! The competition for that vague thing called "control" is often fierce. Often we don't even know what it is we want control of. We just want control! Moreover, power players (aptly called "controllers") mistakenly believe other people provide—or take away—their personal potency. Where do such beliefs come from?

BEGINNINGS OF POWER PLAYS

The roots of adult power players' behavior can often be traced back to childhood. As small children, we fought for power for the first time when, at about age two, we were told in a variety of ways by our parents that it was time to stop being the center of the universe, that cooperation with "the big people" was now necessary. We could remember, we could talk, we could act in socially cooperative ways. If we didn't cooperate, we often were led to believe we'd face punishment or rejection.

When confronted with this commonplace situation, children have three options: They may *rebel, overadapt,* or *cooperate.* Rebels say, "No, I won't go along, and you can't make me," and fight to have what they want in their own way. We've all seen children attempt to overpower and often win over a parent by saying no, holding out, and throwing temper tantrums.

Meanwhile, *overadaptors* are often overpowered by a parent. If, as children, we were overadaptors, we may have developed a feeling of being swallowed up, like our freedom was being stripped away. We may have felt childish grief and fear because our behavior and freedom of choice were being suppressed, not directed. And so we "adapted" and withheld our anger.

Those of us who were guided to become *cooperators,* to recognize that others have needs, too, slowly learned cooperation and that growing up can be a joy. Power sharing and yielding became normal parts of our lives.

There was no need to overpower our parents, nor did they need to overpower us with directives, threats, demands, and physical punishment. Both parent and child can be powerful in their own ways, and in sharing such power, they construct bridges of communication, support, and love. That is normal development. The following story illustrates how the sharing and affirming of equal personal power might have been taught to us as children.

When my daughter Heidi was three, she toddled into the kitchen where I was washing dishes and thinking about the chores I had to complete that evening. "Mommy, read me a story," Heidi said, tugging on my untucked shirt. I looked down, grimacing at the toys scattered across the floor of the kitchen and living room. I thought, Well, I've got time to either read her a story or pick up those toys.

I started to say, "Go pick up your toys and then we'll talk about a story," but I suddenly stopped myself, realizing I would be issuing an irritated order. Instead, I said: "Heidi, I only have time to do one thing: read to you or pick up all those toys. Why don't you decide which thing I should do?"

I had given the child a choice, and Heidi was startled. She had no cause for disappointment or a temper tantrum, because it was her *choice. And she chose; she ran to pick up the toys herself, then returned for the one thing I had time for—reading the story. Getting her to think and choose affirmed her personal power.*

Every one of us, as two- or three-year-old children, moved through a rebellious stage; some of us emerged with few emotional scars, though everyone has some problems with trying to control others. The transition from childish omnipotence to power sharing seems to be something we all struggle with, even in adult life. Our confusion over uses of power is evident in unhealthy, uneasy adult relationships.

ANTIDEPENDENCE

Often accompanying confusion about power is the tendency to mistake *independence* for *antidependence*. To be antidependent is to be uncomfortable with commitment, or to refuse to make any commitment to another at all. In reality, this is the flip side of dependency. Our need to belong is real. People who say "I'll do my thing and you'll do yours, and if we meet, so be it" promote false independence.

I've discovered that most people who exalt their independence in truth fear becoming dependent on others. They've learned to avoid pain and fear by becoming self-sufficient. Control is important to them; they often experienced one or both parents as attempting to overpower them or each other, and so they promised themselves they would never be overpowered. Paradoxically, those control-obsessed parents failed to meet basic developmental needs in the child, and often the child's response was "No, I won't, and you can't make me!" or "I'm okay; you're not!" In this way, the child maintained a sense of personal power and dignity in an uneasy, unhealthy situation.

Sometimes as a result of a parent trying to control our thoughts, feelings, and actions, we learned to be afraid to grant power to others. Our relationships may be characterized by competition, with frequent power games where we fight with a partner for the position of "being right." To power players, giving often feels like loss of power, or giving in.

COMMON POWER PLAYS

What are some of the subtle power plays that sabotage adult love relationships? Below are listed a few of the most common power plays that appear in unhealthy relationships. To the left of each power play, write "yes" or "no" based on whether you have experienced that symptom in your relationship.

In my relationship I have experienced either one of us:

_____ Giving advice, with difficulty taking it

_____ Having difficulty in reaching out and asking for support and love

_____ Giving orders; demanding and expecting too much from the other

_____ Trying to "get even" or to diminish the self-esteem or power of the other

_____ Tending to be judgmental; making putdowns that sabotage the other's success; fault finding; persecuting; punishing

_____ "Holding out" on the other; not giving what the other wants or needs

_____ Making, then breaking promises; seducing into trust

_____ Smothering, over-nurturing the other: "Big Daddy," "Mama Bird"

_____ Patronizing, condescending treatment of the other that sets one partner up as superior and the other as inferior; intimidating

_____ Making decisions for the other; discounting the other's ability to problem solve

_____ Difficulty admitting mistakes or saying "I'm sorry"

_____ Giving indirect, evasive answers to questions

_____ Manipulating to put other in "no-win" situations

_____ Attempting to change the other (and unwillingness to change the self)

_____ "Pouring salt in the wounds"—attacking the other when he or she is most vulnerable

_____ Showing an antidependent attitude: "I don't need you"

_____ Using bullying, bribing behavior; using threats

_____ Showing bitterness, grudge holding, or feeling self-righteous anger

_____ Using verbal or physical abuse

_____ Using aggression defined as assertion

_____ Needing to win or be right

_____ Showing stubborn resistance or being set in own ways

_____ Defending any of the above behaviors

How many "yes" answers do you have? How many "no's"? Compare. Since power plays are characteristic of unhealthy dependency, any "yes" indicates some problems. The more times you write "yes," the more attention you'll want to pay to the presence of such harmful manipulation and control by either one of the partners in your relationship. Keep in mind that power plays are not usually in our awareness.

To feel powerful, one person must overwhelm and control the other; the power player has difficulty sharing power for fear of being overpowered. What such a person is really saying and does not realize is this: "I fear I'm powerless and I need to control others so I can be powerful." Such a false belief suggests another person is in charge of our personal potency, and that we need to control that other person in order to be secure and strong.

The power player struggles to keep others in a victim's position so they can be rescued or persecuted. Such melodramatics are not the essence of true personal power, but of dependency; they are most surely unhealthy. Ultimately, power plays are the cause of much unhappiness.

Power plays are not easily given up by either participant, for they mask unconscious and often suppressed fears. In each incidence where I have explored the roots of a client's need to control another person, I've found that a traumatic experience or imagined threat has led this person to interpret loss of control as the *loss of self,* a dangerous and terrifying idea. Or perhaps power players were allowed to overpower their parents, thus developing a belief that "I am more powerful than you and I can get my own way."

"Besides," reasoned one power player, "being 'one-up' feels much better than being 'one-down,' so why give up behavior that makes me feel good?" People striving to control others can avoid dealing with their own private fears, insecurities, and doubts because they always have someone else who is "less okay" to focus on. Keep in mind that power plays are mutual. The victim's position often has its perceived benefits, too! It is safe and predictable and keeps others around. The "one-down" participant, who is being controlled by a partner, fears rejection or angry confrontation and unhappily complies. The people who play these power games fail to recognize that both positions are unstable and unhealthy; both are based on false beliefs.

Because we may have designed our own power plays when we were children to protect us from harm, they are deeply embedded behaviors, and our resistance to giving them up will be very great.

Because "one-up" power players dominate others by delusion and denial, believing they are better than others, they seldom reach out for help or indicate they want to change. Generally, they are forced into therapy or change when they experience a trauma, such as the partner's threat to leave. Even then, their primary goal may be to regain control over the rebellious partner.

At this point, the partner usually is no longer willing to be a victim; sometimes he or she may be angry and may even begin fierce competition for that "one-up" position. If this is the case, neither partner is ready to give up the power plays until the insecurities that motivate them have been explored. Perhaps this is fear of pain or deprivation; fear of disappointing someone; fear of failure; fear of guilt, anger, or rejection; fear of being alone; fear of getting sick or going crazy; even fear of death.

WHAT ARE OUR OPTIONS?

Once we identify the power plays sabotaging our relationships, we have three options.

First, we could cooperate and respond passively from a victim's position, agreeing to forfeit our own potency and accept the "one-down" position. It is easy and familiar, even though addictive. Needless to say, this is no way to live fully. Yet many people choose this stance. I find it curious that those who live in a constant "one-down" position usually end up with the feelings the other partner is trying to avoid.

Second, we could seek the power position, in which case we become snared in a competitive, addictive relationship. In this case, two *anti*dependent people vie for the "one-up" position, living in constant conflict as each tries to overwhelm the other with creative and destructive power play tactics.

Unfortunately, most relationships alternate between these two options, seesawing through life! There's a third, much happier option, however. That is to respond from an affirmative position which acknowledges *equal personal power*. From this position we are saying, "We are both okay and personally powerful. Sometimes it is your behavior that is not acceptable to me."

When we adopt this attitude, it's important for us to recognize how power plays have victimized both partners in our relationships. We can then work to nurture a new sense of personal power and dignity for us both.

WITHDRAWING FROM POWER PLAYS

To withdraw ourselves from power plays we need to do the following:

- acknowledge that power plays are real
- take an inventory of the power plays we most often participate in

- learn to identify our own personal cues: feeling confused, trapped, guilty, uncomfortable, threatened, competitive; doubting ourselves; using sarcasm; being defensive; projecting blame; avoiding our partners; giving evasive responses
- examine our negative personal beliefs that are supporting power plays, and change them
- detach ourselves, maintaining a belief that we are equals

During the struggle to break free of power plays, you may find yourself ensnared in arguments caused by the power-seeking behavior of your partner. The less you say in response to verbal challenges, the better. The urge to defend yourself or to agree can lead you directly back into unhealthy behavior. Thus, short, one-word responses are most effective in order to stay detached from power competition: "yes," "no," "whatever," or "really" are examples. Or you may choose to let go and make a nonthreatening statement of your position to affirm your dignity. An example of this is a statement such as, "When you . . . [action], I feel . . . [feeling]." You are responding from a position of equal personal power. Make this statement at a time you are most likely to be heard, not during an argument. Following is an example of a couple who are moving toward a healthier relationship based on each partner's equal personal power.

THE GOAL: MUTUAL RESPECT

Jennifer and Brad had a potentially good relationship. But Brad was obsessed with his role as rescuer and adviser to many people, a role indicative of one trying to hold power over others. Thus Brad had many "victim" friends demanding his time and energy, people Jennifer called "hangers-on," and not true friends. Though Brad often complained these people ate up his time, he also said he could not say no to them.

Jennifer often felt neglected and lonely, but she said little for several years, always hoping the situation would change. Her style, one she had learned from her family, was to say nothing and feel bad. Since she had not experienced power sharing in her family, her fear of confronting Brad, and possibly causing him to grow angry and reject her, was very real.

When she finally gathered the courage to confront him, she did so with great feeling and honesty. She told Brad she was no longer willing to postpone her own needs for those of his acquaintances, saying, "When you cancel our weekend plans because a friend wants you to help him move, I feel unimportant to you, hurt, and very angry." She had begun to recognize that her behavior was a pattern carried over from childhood, when she had often bowed to the needs of others in her family. She no longer wanted to do this.

At first, Brad listened sympathetically; later he verbally attacked Jennifer, accusing her of manipulating him with tears and trying to control their relationship. To regain his equilibrium, Brad began to criticize her, withhold affection from her, and lecture her on how their marriage "should and would" be from then on.

Jennifer knew she could comply, stand and affirm her personal dignity, or leave the marriage. Fortunately, she was strong enough to recognize that although Brad's behavior hurt her, it stemmed from his *fear of losing control and being hurt himself*. Determined not to stay a victim, Jennifer managed to maintain detachment and not take his criticism personally.

When opportune times arose, she told Brad how his behavior affected her, although she knew she could not realistically expect to change him. She also made it clear she wanted a healthy marriage where both of them could contribute their own thoughts, feelings, and ways of doing things as equals, without fear of reprisal. Jennifer hoped such an ideal could be achieved; if it couldn't, she would have no choice but to consider how or if she would remain in this relationship.

Fortunately, both Jennifer and Brad are now working to achieve a stronger, freer relationship. It hasn't been easy for them; but an improving atmosphere of mutual respect has allowed them to move from a controlling, dependent relationship to one that supports—yet frees—them both. The power plays are less frequent, and they are better for that—individually and as a couple.

POWER WITHIN

Winning is an internal process: power is within ourselves and results in self-confidence, self-love, and a desire to give to another. With a sense of confidence, we no longer need to "win" externally. Our chances of achieving fulfillment in a healthy love relationship increase when we finally realize power need not be something one person has at another's expense.

I continue to be amazed at how frequently people begin getting what they want and need in relationships *as soon as they are willing to give up the need for power and control*. Perhaps it is because each senses that the other partner's power lies confidently within, and in awe and respect, is moved to reach out and give. Or perhaps it is as Daniel Travanti, the actor, said control over others is an illusion, and the answer is in letting go. Yielding is a sign of wellness. In a storm, it is the tree that bends with the wind that survives to grow tall.

WORKING THROUGH CONFLICT

Brian DesRoches

In recovery from codependency, we're challenged to develop healthy ways of relating to others. Often, we'll face our greatest challenges as we learn and test new skills for resolving conflict. Conflict can present us with some of our most fearful and uncomfortable experiences. Even thinking about the potential of conflict is enough to make some of us feel tense and anxious. In the past, we probably either withdrew from conflict or attacked out of fear, thus reinforcing unhealthy patterns of conflict resolution we may have learned in our family.

When we reflect on our family, we can often identify two ineffective ways conflicts were resolved: (1) avoidance and denial, or (2) explosive and harmful anger. Consequently, many of the ways we learned to resolve

Reprinted, with changes, with permission of Hazelden Foundation. From *Working Through Conflict*, by Brian DesRoches. Copyright © 1990, by Brian DesRoches.

conflicts are ineffective at alleviating stress and anxiety and at building healthy relationships. Some of the behaviors we may have used include these:

- *denial*—distancing ourselves from conflict by refusing to acknowledge it
- *capitulation*—giving up and allowing ourselves to be victims of a conflict
- *withdrawal*—pulling away from conflict because of hurt feelings, anger, frustration, or resentment
- *shaming*—putting another person down by attacking or discounting his or her character, motives, judgment, or feelings
- *emotional cutoff*—stopping all communication with a person in an attempt to change his or her behavior
- *threats*—making ultimatums that demand a change in another person's behavior
- *humor and sarcasm*—using jokes and cutting remarks to shift the focus off the conflict
- *manipulation*—using guilt-provoking statements, competitiveness, or deceit to avoid or win a conflict

As we work through our recovery program, we'll discover the various ways we have tried to control people with whom we have had conflicts. Recovery is a process of unlearning unhealthy behaviors and learning healthy ways of coping and dealing with conflict. Very few of us learned healthy conflict resolution in our family. We may not have learned how to

- negotiate and express needs
- establish and maintain personal boundaries

- listen to another person's concerns
- deal with our feelings
- respect and be comfortable with differences among ourselves and others

Recovery gives us the opportunity to learn these new relationship skills.

How We Lost Touch with Ourselves

In our family, we developed beliefs and perceptions about conflict and the harm it can cause us. Consequently, some of us may avoid conflict at all costs; others of us may become so entangled in it that we leave ourselves vulnerable to emotional or physical abuse. We may have even abused others in our attempts to resolve a conflict.

In *Codependent No More,* Melody Beattie defines a codependent person as "one who has let another person's behavior affect him or her, and who is obsessed with controlling that person's behavior."* This description gives us some clues about how we lost touch with ourselves. We lost touch by focusing on the other person and acting out controlling behaviors such as withdrawal, submission, aggression, denial, and avoidance. Over time, these controlling responses became automatic when we perceived a conflict. We paid a high price in lost self-esteem and physical and emotional stress.

In recovery, it's natural for us to feel confused about how to resolve conflict. But through our recovery pro-

---

* Melody Beattie, *Codependent No More* (Center City, Minn.:Hazelden Educational Materials, 1987), 31.

gram, we can develop new skills for resolving conflict that will honor ourselves and other people. Recovery presents us with the opportunity to gain more control over our responses to conflict while focusing less on trying to control the behavior of other people. This is new territory for us, but it's a place where we can grow.

In this pamphlet, we'll look at how we can develop new ways of resolving conflict in our life. We'll see how some people developed new tools for conflict resolution, and we'll explore what they learned about themselves in the process. Most important, we'll examine how they changed the perceptions that caused them to feel threatened by conflict.

TOWARD NEW WAYS OF HANDLING CONFLICT

Recovery from codependency involves developing healthy ways of expressing our feelings and resolving the conflicts that are a part of living and working with others. We *can* change. And every conflict *can* be a source of learning and healing. Even our conflicts with loved ones and friends can help us learn to let go and trust in the process of our recovery.

The origins of our conflicts are often rooted in issues we seldom discuss, including our need for safety, security, recognition, love, respect, and acceptance. As we work through our conflicts, we'll not only develop healthier ways of living and relating, we'll also be healing the wounded parts of us that we've ignored for so long.

Our Body's Response to Conflict

Our body has a built-in alarm system that prepares us for conflict. This system begins to operate even when we think about or sense a potential for conflict. We usually experience potential conflict as a physical state of tension, stress, restlessness, and anxiety. Our body is preparing to fight or withdraw. This has often been described as "walking on eggs." Emotionally, we may feel distrustful, cautious, threatened, and fearful. Then, in the midst of conflict, we often feel angry, resentful, rejected, and defensive. We will react with various forms of fighting or withdrawing, neither of which provides us with effective resolution of conflict.

Our emotional state resulting from an actual or potential conflict is a natural part of the body's stress response. For any conflict to cause an emotional reaction, we must first perceive it as a threat to our values, self-esteem, self-image, beliefs, or sense of physical and emotional safety.

Each of us has a different perception of what is threatening. For some of us, a loud voice can cause us to feel threatened; for others of us, a difference of opinion can have the same impact. We may find that our conflict alarm is set off by how others look, the way they dress, the expression on a person's face, or even a pointed finger.

What Sets Off Our Conflict Alarm?

In some situations, our conflict alarm goes off because of critical judgments we've made about other people. In other situations, our conflict alarm goes off because of behaviors and beliefs we learned in our family of origin. The all-or-none, black-or-white, right-or-wrong thinking that is a part of our codependency often forms the basis for the judgments we make of others.

When we are not open to how other people perceive things or when our thinking puts other people in one box or another (good or bad, thoughtful or thoughtless, cooperative or uncooperative), then we are stuck. We lose our flexibility and will be threatened by anything that doesn't fit into our predefined thinking of the way things should be.

Not only do the judgments we make of other people and the unhealthy behaviors and beliefs we learned in our family create stress for us, they also cut us off from learning healthy ways to resolve conflict. The feelings caused by a conflict, or even the perception of a conflict, can become so overpowering that we lose our ability to think clearly and focus on resolving the conflict. We lose touch with ourselves and our feelings.

As recovering codependents, we're likely to deny and avoid our feelings, especially those about conflict. In recovery, we can work through these feelings in positive ways. As in our recovery program, awareness and acceptance—and admitting we are powerless over controlling the behavior of others—are the first steps toward making changes in our life. All our efforts at conflict resolution will be hampered unless we become aware of, accept, and deal with our feelings.

A look at Tom's work situation shows us how important it is to identify our feelings. Tom is a laboratory technician in the research department of a major chemical manufacturer. Although he enjoys his work, his relationship with his boss, Barry, has been a source of conflict.

Tom:

Before starting my recovery from codependency, I often didn't know when I was having a conflict with someone. I'd just do what seemed natural to me—when I was angry at someone I'd try to get back at him or her. Most of the time I didn't even know I was doing this or how it affected me. I just did it.

At work, I didn't like how upset and powerless I felt. Sometimes, I'd be in a staff meeting and I'd ignore Barry or try to get him to ask me a lot of questions about my work. Other times, I'd be damned if I'd talk about anything with him unless I had to.

I was stuck in the same old way of reacting to Barry. I had to become aware of my feelings and deal with them before I could even think about talking with him.

Like many of us, Tom learned during recovery that he was reacting from patterns that he had learned in his family. Our family and personal relationships, because of their intimate nature, are areas in which conflict can easily develop. We can probably think of many conflicts we have had with friends, lovers, spouses, parents, or children.

Jason and Kathy have been married twelve years and have two children, ages nine and six. Their story shows how conflict is often handled in an intimate relationship in which both members are codependent. Jason withdrew during conflict. Kathy pursued Jason as he withdrew. This became their conflict style. They often became so caught up in their conflicts that they lost track of the reason for the disagreement. Prior to beginning recovery, they were unable to tolerate differences in each other. They were stuck in cycles of withdrawal and pursuit.

Kathy:

We dealt with conflict in one of two ways. Either we didn't talk about things or I got loud and upset and pushed Jason to do and see things my way. He was the passive one; I was the aggressive one.

Jason:

When we didn't talk about our feelings, it was like we had formed a pact not to make each other upset. But it was all so invisible that even we didn't know it until we started recovery. It was like "out of sight, out of mind." But it was still there and we both felt it.

Acting out of Childhood Pain

Recognition, acceptance, love, respect, and feeling physically and emotionally safe—these are needs we all share. If these needs were not met in childhood, they can become the sources of adult conflicts as we, consciously or unconsciously, try to get others to meet them for us. But, as we learn in recovery, each of us is responsible for communicating and meeting our needs in healthy ways. Effective conflict resolution grows out of the acknowledgment that while we cannot make anyone meet our needs, we can communicate what they are.

In recovery, Kathy and Jason began focusing more on their feelings about what the other said or did. This made a big difference in their relationship and their recovery. Jason realized that beneath his passive resistance were deep despair and loneliness, feelings he had covered up as a child and avoided as an adult. Kathy began to understand how her aggressive reaction to Jason's behavior kept her from feeling the fear and abandonment that had its origin in her childhood. With this awareness she was able to start making changes in the way she expressed her feelings. Together, they learned two of the keys to resolving conflict: *self-awareness* and *self-focus*.

Kathy:

I feel more intimate with Jason. We both are learning to express our feelings without getting caught up in the emotions of our conflicts. It has taken a lot of self-awareness to focus on my own reactions in a healthy way, but it works.

As recovering codependents, many of us have had difficulty with conflict because we are susceptible to taking on the emotions of those around us. But by paying attention to our internal reactions to a situation, we become aware of our feelings and are able to assess and express them in healthy ways. When Tom, Kathy, and Jason began focusing on their physical and emotional reactions to conflict, it was the beginning of change for them.

Listening to Our Body and the Voices Inside

There are some things we can do to help us become aware of our feelings and express them in healthy ways. First, we can pay attention to our body and our breathing. When we get into a conflict, our breathing often becomes shallow and rapid. Our pulse quickens, and we may sweat. When we feel our body reacting this way, we know this is a time to stop action. We can stop to focus on our feelings *before* we react from old patterns. Some people count to ten or one hundred before they think about what action to take.

We can also listen to what the voices in our mind are saying. We can ask, *What messages am I giving myself? Why am I feeling this way?* We often don't notice this inner dialogue, the ongoing "chatter" in our minds about what we think is right and wrong and what the other person should or should not do, but it's a catalyst for many of our reactions to conflict. It's part of codependent *either/or* thinking.

When Tom obsessed about his conflict with Barry, he didn't pay attention to his body, and he was unable to pay attention to the messages he gave himself. He was unaware of the powerful internal dialogue that influenced his reactions to conflict.

Tom:

When I finally stopped acting out my side of the conflict and focused on my feelings, I could hear the little messages I was giving myself like, He can't treat me like that; I'll show him! *and* Why is he doing that to me? *I was constantly replaying Barry's behavior in my mind and getting more and*

*more angry. No wonder I was always worked up
and unable to let go.*

When we stop action for a while, we give ourselves
time to think about what we are doing, what we want to
do about the conflict, and what our choices are. At first,
Jason felt frustrated when he tried this.

Jason:
   *I was able to stop action and listen to myself, but
   I didn't know what to do next. In my family we didn't
   learn how to handle conflict. Here I was, thirty-eight
   years old, still not knowing what to say when I was in
   a conflict with Kathy.*

Jason then took the next step after focusing on himself. He thought about what he wanted, what the conflict was about, and what he could do to resolve it.

Jason:
   *Before starting to work on how to resolve conflict,
   I'd just withdraw. Now I ask myself,* What do I want
   and how can I express my needs so Kathy will hear
   me? *It's like learning a new language, but I'm learning it.*

With the support of their marriage counselor, Jason
and Kathy developed a list of questions to ask themselves and each other to help them deal with their conflicts. Some of these questions were:

• What opinions do we each have on the issue?
• What does it mean to me if I don't get what I want?

• How have we settled similar differences in the past?
• What are our options?

Asking these questions helped Kathy and Jason learn about their differences. Both of them saw how their fear of differences of opinion and values often resulted in conflict.

When Tom began thinking about how he could change his interaction with Barry, he realized how frustrating and tiring it would be to continue focusing on changing Barry. So he let go of trying to change Barry and changed himself.

Tom:

At first I didn't like being the one who had to change. I kept telling myself that he had to change too. But when I realized that I could relieve my stress and frustration, I decided it was worth it to try new ways of relating to Barry. It's been a challenge because a part of me still wants to change him, but now I know I don't have to listen to that part of me as much.

Letting Go of Trying to Change Other People

One of the greatest challenges we'll face in learning how to resolve conflict is letting go of trying to change the person with whom we are having a conflict. Trying to change the behavior, feelings, or thoughts of another person is a primary characteristic of codependency. This behavior keeps us from focusing on feelings of powerlessness and other painful feelings that may be influencing our behavior. None of us want to feel emotional pain, especially leftover hurt from our childhood. But we're only able to let go of trying to change other people when we accept our powerlessness over them and are willing to surrender the outcome of our conflicts to our Higher Power. For example, as Kathy accepted the ways she was trying to control Jason, she felt the deep hurt and fear of abandonment she had been avoiding since she was a child. Then, with practice, she was able to let go of trying to change Jason. She began accepting him and trusting her Higher Power with the outcome of their conflicts. This is the essence of recovery: to let go and let others be themselves as we are ourselves.

We can take time to reflect on our role in a conflict and what we can do to change our behavior. Some of the questions we can ask ourselves include these:

- What am I telling myself to do about this conflict and the other person?
- What is the way I think things should be?
- Am I taking responsibility for my feelings and thoughts, or am I expecting the other person to change?
- Are my thoughts making me think like a victim or like someone who can negotiate conflict?

SALT TALKS

The strategy Tom, Jason, and Kathy used to learn new conflict resolution skills is called SALT, which stands for Stop Action, Listen, and Think. During a conflict, this strategy can help you:

- Stop Action for a moment so you can focus on your body and feelings and breathe deeply and slowly. This will help you get your bearings so you can stop focusing on others and their behavior. In any conflict, you first need to stop action and focus on yourself *before* you can make beneficial changes.
- Listen to your self-talk. Are you telling yourself to change the other person and get him or her to see your side? Do you feel afraid or threatened? Listening to yourself will help you become aware of your thoughts and feelings about a conflict.
- Think about what you want to do. You can change your usual ways of reacting by thinking about your choices. This step can give you a feeling of mastery over your actions and the confidence to deal effectively with conflict.

UNDERSTANDING THE SOURCES OF OUR CONFLICTS

Changing the way we react to conflict also helps us examine the sources of our conflicts. We are sometimes unaware of our reasons for being upset. When we understand the roots of our reactions to conflict, we are better able to control our responses, heal ourselves, and identify our needs for safety, recognition, love, respect, and acceptance.

For example, how we perceive a person's behavior or words has a significant influence on how we relate to that person. If we perceive that a person will ignore one of our needs, then a conflict will probably develop. But we are not always aware of our perceptions, particularly if we are focusing on the other person in a conflict. Although we can't always know why we perceive things the way we do, we can become aware of our perceptions and how they create conflict for us.

For example, Tom's perceptions of Barry created problems in their relationship.

Tom:

I thought he was an inconsiderate jerk who wouldn't pay attention to the good work I did. It was a constant battle to get him to acknowledge my work and listen to me. I thought he should know his employees' needs and give us the recognition we deserve.

It would be hard to pinpoint exactly why Tom perceived Barry the way he did, but two things are clear: (1) Tom's conflict with Barry was largely based on Tom's expectation of how a boss should behave, and (2) Tom wanted recognition from Barry and tried hard to get it.

Tom:

I created the conflict with Barry out of my need for him to acknowledge the good work I was doing. It seemed he was ignoring me just like my father did, and I wasn't going to let him get away with it. My need for recognition caused a lot of problems. Now, I may not always get what I need from Barry, but I don't have to feel so powerless over the situation. I can look at my role in the conflict and change myself.

Tom could have gone on believing that it was Barry who was at fault for their conflicts. Tied up in his codependency, Tom could have created even more stress for himself. Instead, Tom chose to look at himself and his role in the conflict.

Letting Go of Obsessive Thinking

Many of us have experienced similar situations with co-workers or supervisors. Caught in our codependency, we often obsess about the other person's behavior and how to change it. This only increases our anxiety and tension, and leaves us with few options for resolving the conflict. By obsessing, we

- give other people the power to make us miserable
- cause stress and conflict for ourselves
- are unable to determine what we need to do to resolve the conflict at hand
- are unable to develop a sense of control over our life

By letting go of our obsessive thinking, we

- release tension and discomfort
- free up mental energy to focus on other options for conflict resolution
- are able to develop a sense of control over our life

After using the tools mentioned in this pamphlet to discover the sources of their conflicts, Jason and Kathy learned something new about themselves. Jason realized how important feeling respected and appreciated was to him. Kathy discovered how important it was for her to feel financially secure. Money and general security were significant factors in her conflicts with Jason. Other conflicts developed when one of them perceived that his or her needs were not being acknowledged or when one of them felt threatened by the other. Neither of them had recognized this until they began recovering from codependency.

Kathy:

In all our years of marriage, I never told Jason that I needed to feel financially secure. I didn't even know it myself until we began to talk about our separate values and needs and how they created conflict in our marriage. I would get upset and would argue with Jason whenever we had money problems. If I'd never looked at the source of this conflict, I may have never known about my needs. I can see how my childhood and the difficulties my family had with money had a lot of influence on my thinking.

By taking time to explore the sources of their conflicts and changing themselves, Tom, Kathy, and Jason discovered that *if we believe that the sources of our conflicts are other people, we are caught in the codependent trap of having to change the other person to resolve any conflict.*

Questions to Ask Yourself

Ask yourself the following questions when you are in a conflict. They will help you understand the source of the conflict and your role in it.

Question:
Is this a conflict over personal values and beliefs?

You may find yourself having a conflict over how you believe a person should treat you. Instead of reacting out of anger, you can explain your need to that person.

Question:
Does the conflict involve a threat to my body or my self-image?

A direct threat to your body will stimulate your conflict alarm and a strong reaction to protect yourself. You may have a similar response when someone criticizes you. When you are aware that you feel threatened, you can stop to assess the reality of the threat and then decide on your action.

Question:
Is the conflict about my need for recognition, acceptance, or a sense of personal freedom?

Conflicts with people in positions of authority or with people we're very close to are often related to these needs. It's natural and human to seek recognition, acceptance, or a sense of personal freedom. Yet we can seldom attain these through conflict. We can decide how to express our needs to those involved and discover what we can do to take care of ourselves and our feelings if these needs will not be met by the other person.

Question:

What are my perceptions of the other person's behavior and what role have my perceptions played in determining my feelings and in causing the conflict?

Answering this question helps us discover the behavior to which we are having a reaction.

Question:

What needs do I want met by the person with whom I am having a conflict? (This could include recognition, respect, safety, love, acceptance, or acknowledgment.)

This question helps us discover what we want from the other person. When we discover this, we can ask for what we need. This doesn't mean we'll always get it, but it does show that we assume responsibility for meeting our needs.

NONJUDGMENTAL THINKING

Jason:

Now I can see what I have been doing that's unhealthy, but how can I act differently? I never learned how to negotiate a conflict or even how to express my needs.

Tom:

I can use the SALT strategy, but what then? I've got to say something or act differently if I'm really going to recover.

Many of us have had similar feelings in recovery. We become aware of something we want to change but don't know how to do it. In conflict negotiations, we can use new, nonjudgmental patterns of communication. We have already learned that dealing with feelings first is the key. A nonjudgmental approach to conflict resolution allows both people in a conflict to have their feelings and opinions. Dealing with these differences up front can help to make them easier to accept. This is unlike our old approach to conflict resolution where we didn't accept other people's feelings and opinions but attempted to change them.

Developing a nonjudgmental approach to conflict resolution is a part of letting go of control, which is a part of our recovery process. We need to avoid making quick judgments because as soon as we make a judgment about how people should behave, we attempt to control them. This doesn't mean that we shouldn't judge whether or not a person's behavior is safe for us. We need to protect ourselves. But we also need to recognize that we can't change another person's behavior.

Being nonjudgmental doesn't mean that we deny our hurt feelings or anger, but we express our feelings without placing blame on the other person. This is an important expression of nonjudgmental thinking.

We also need to acknowledge the other person's feelings without trying to change them. Otherwise, even if we have used the SALT technique and feel we have been nonjudgmental, the other person may still feel upset and tense. Talking rationally about our needs to a person who is upset or fearful can be frustrating. Tom had this experience when he tried to talk to Barry about his need for recognition.

Tom:

I felt ready to talk to Barry, but he got upset when I started to discuss it with him. So I just tried harder to discuss it with him, forgetting that he probably had feelings, too, and didn't have the benefit of a recovery program. I could have handled it better by acknowledging his feelings as we were talking.

Some Tips on Healthy Ways to Express Our Feelings

Throughout this chapter we have talked about how important it is to express our feelings. This is usually easier said than done. For some of us, just the thought of talking about our feelings is uncomfortable. But we can acknowledge how awkward and uncomfortable we feel about expressing ourselves. When it comes to conflict resolution, we can follow a few tips that will help us express our feelings in healthy ways.

Tip:
Use simple, responsible communication to let the other person know how you feel about his or her behavior.

Instead of saying "You make me feel _____," we can say, "When you [describe the behavior], I feel _____."

Tip:
Stay with your feelings and avoid interpreting the other person's thoughts, words, feelings, or behavior.

For example, avoid saying things such as "You're angry, aren't you?" Instead, describe what you are observing, and ask, "Your body looks tense. Are you angry?"

Tip:
If you feel attacked or hurt by another person's use of the word "you," (for example, "You don't know what you're talking about. . . .''), you don't have to respond defensively.

Instead, ask the person about the impact of your behavior by asking, "Have my comments upset you?" We can take responsibility for our communication and change it if necessary.

Tip:
Knowing when to express our feelings is an important part of conflict resolution.

We can make a conflict more frustrating for ourselves by seeking resolution when the other person is distracted or busy. Asking for time to share feelings and resolve a conflict is an important part of the skills we are learning.

*   *   *

After expressing our feelings, we can focus on two other fundamental aspects of conflict resolution: (1) the issues from our perspective, and (2) the issues from the other person's perspective. It's helpful at this stage to define the problem in terms of what issues need to be resolved and what needs are to be met. Jason and Kathy learned a lot about each other as they began to express the needs underlying their conflicts. Kathy realized that Jason had a side of him that she had never known.

Kathy:

I discovered that when I focused on me and expressed my need for financial security, Jason revealed his need to feel respected by me and acknowledged for what he had done for the family. I always thought he knew that I respected and appreciated him, but I found out that he didn't know for sure. We began to discuss ways to get our needs met, but it took practice and time.

When Tom and his boss sat down to discuss their conflict, Tom was able to ask Barry, in a direct and nonthreatening manner, for the kind of feedback he needed to feel like he was part of the team in the lab.

Tom:

Even though Barry said he couldn't give me all the feedback I wanted, he did agree to a regular monthly meeting to review my work and the projects I was interested in. I felt good about that. What a difference!

Things were different for Tom, Kathy, and Jason because they worked their recovery programs and looked at how they created conflict and blocked effective negotiation. They also learned a key aspect of successful conflict negotiation: respect for themselves and others.

SUMMARY

In a conflict we are often blinded by fear and overcome by our feelings. And while we may still feel fearful and overwhelmed, we don't have to act out of our old patterns of denial, avoidance, capitulation, control, or domination. We know that these are unhealthy alternatives that won't help us build the self-esteem and trusting relationships we seek. Instead, we can respect ourselves and others as we negotiate conflicts. When we use the SALT technique and practice being nonjudgmental, we are being respectful to ourselves and others.

Writer and philosopher Aldous Huxley wrote, "Experience is not what happens to you but what you make of what happens to you." Before we started recovery, we may have thought conflict was something that happened to us, something we had to avoid or struggle to control.

Now, by focusing on ourselves in conflict situations, we can take steps to learn about our needs and change the codependent patterns we have used to try to get them met. Conflicts *can* be a source of growth for us. Believe it or not, we can even become grateful for the conflicts we have had and will have. Each conflict is an opportunity to let go a little more, to learn something new about ourselves, and to strengthen our skills at conflict resolution.

Growing in our ability to resolve conflict is closely linked to growing in our recovery. We can practice using our recovery tools in conflict situations. As we begin to focus on ourselves and our reactions, and surrender our need to control others, our ability to work through conflicts is greatly enhanced. As we strengthen the belief in our ability to resolve conflicts, our life becomes more expressive and creative. We feel less inhibited by our fears. We grow in recovery as we begin to see the conflicts in our lives as a way of healing and expressing our love to others.

FORGIVENESS

Stephanie Abbott

And throughout all eternity
I forgive you, you forgive me
—WILLIAM BLAKE

Forgiveness is a path to personal power and peace. By practicing forgiveness daily, we can replace resentment with the warmth of positive feelings for others. We can replace faultfinding with harmony. "Only the brave know how to forgive," wrote eighteenth-century British novelist Laurence Sterne. For some of us, it's the hardest thing we will ever do.

A member of Al-Anon once commented, "I needed to find a way to love my husband without pain." She found that way through forgiveness of the past, a quality that made a vast difference in her life. But she was the one who had made a shift in her feelings; the people around her were still the same. Her change in attitude gave her great insight into the power of full forgiveness.

We can't be pressured to forgive before we're ready, but the intent to forgive can make us feel better imme-

Reprinted, with changes, with permission of Hazelden Foundation. From *Forgiveness: The Power and the Process*, by Stephanie Abbott. Copyright © 1989, by Hazelden Foundation.

diately. It gives us time to get through the hurt and anger, as we become willing to be ready to forgive sometime in the future.

When we suffer from a relationship with a dysfunctional person, we need to learn how to take care of ourselves. Part of that new learning is to tell the difference between forgiveness and tolerating mistreatment. *Forgiveness* will help us let go of our pain from the past. *Tolerating mistreatment* will invite more of the same and increase our burden of shame.

When we forgive, we release blame and anger regarding a person who has hurt or disappointed us. We reach the end of grief, and we feel the willingness to let go.

Why would we want to forgive someone who has hurt us? Isn't forgiveness letting that person off the hook or saying that our pain isn't that important?

I believe forgiveness is good because it's practical: we benefit from it. It frees us from the acts that hurt us, so we can get on with our lives. It frees us from struggles to manipulate or change other people. It frees us from the futile struggles of retaliation. It frees us to feel our own personal power in our lives.

Anger uses energy and exhausts us. Forgiveness, by contrast, empowers us with vigor and spirit to nurture the qualities that can enrich our lives. One of the best personal benefits is the serenity we feel after forgiveness. We have better things to do with our lives than to brood over the behavior of other people. As the popular saying goes, "Living well is the best revenge."

Yet, as we realize the personal benefits of forgiveness, we should also realize that it is a process that takes time. Sometimes we think we have forgiven someone, only to have hurt and resentment about the past flare up again. This doesn't mean we haven't forgiven; it means that the process is not yet complete.

It is easier to forgive others when we understand ourselves. This chapter will give us the tools needed to better understand ourselves, and when we recognize codependent behaviors in ourselves, to begin the process of forgiveness. It will show us how letting go of grudges and resentments against ourselves and others will give us much personal power. It will show us a way, through forgiveness, to love others without pain.

Jennifer's Story: *"I feel comfortable giving. I don't know how to do anything else."*

"I call myself a codependent. When I read a list of codependent traits, it sounds like me. But I'm not sure yet what I need to do about it. My father was a seaman. He was home long enough to father six children but not long enough to be a parent. When he retired and was home all the time, his alcoholism became too stressful for the family to cope with. My mother divorced him with the complete approval of all of us grown children.

"Today, at twenty-six, I'm the supervisor of a nursing home, and I'm working on my master's in business administration. I've been married to two alcoholics, and now I'm living with a recovering cocaine addict. I know I'm very successful at managing people, and I feel good about my achievements and future.

"On the other hand, there's no one I feel close to. I know how to help people and to give them support. But that's not the same as having friends I can turn to. I feel comfortable giving. I don't know how to do anything else."

Jennifer has identified some of the traits that we associate with codependency. She is proud of her ability to control herself and her environment. But her extreme self-reliance has meant she can never permit others to help her. Her style is to caretake others without knowing her own needs. She doesn't trust anyone, and being close to someone makes her very anxious unless she can be in charge. She typically fills her time with projects and can't relax enough to play. When asked about her happiness, she says she doesn't think about it. When further questioned, she will reluctantly admit she often feels depressed, but she doesn't like to dwell on her feelings.

Many people can identify with Jennifer. Her traits form a pattern that we call codependency:

- controlling
- caretaking
- neglecting herself
- pushing away her feelings and anxiety
- having relationships with addicts

These strong codependency traits may make forgiveness especially challenging for Jennifer and others like her.

SPECIAL DIFFICULTIES FOR CODEPENDENTS

Let's examine seven traits that are often identified with codependency and see how they affect the process of forgiveness.

- Control
- Frozen Feelings
- External Reference
- Confused Identity
- Low Self-Esteem
- Caretaking
- Perfectionism

Control

Some of us who identify with codependency issues find that we base too much of our self-worth on the mistaken belief that we're responsible for others' good behavior. When others behave badly toward us, the blow is doubly painful. Not only have we been hurt by the behavior, but we berate ourselves as if we think it's our fault that the other person acted this way. Forgiveness means letting go of what happened while changing the grandiose idea that we can control the thinking and behavior of other people. Letting go of this grandiosity gives us the chance to feel better about ourselves, since we no longer feel that someone else's conduct reflects on us.

Joyce's Story: *"I've noticed I have a tendency to want to improve people in general."*

"I know now that a lot of my suffering comes from what I tell myself. I have four grown children, and one of them is an addict. Sometimes he is better, but then he relapses again. My husband and I are active in our church and raised our children with love. We are a close family and still do things together. This one son stays away from us for months, and then I know he's in trouble again. When he comes to family gatherings, sometimes he's fine. But other times, even when he's sober, he blames us for all his problems. It's really hard to listen to his anger, not only because I love my son but because I can slip into blaming myself since I can't make him well.

"I'm learning in Al-Anon that I'm only responsible for how *I* respond, not what he does. It's helped me to sort out what I have control over and what I don't. It's made it so much easier to forgive him for what he says when I don't carry so much self-blame.

"It's been so good for me to learn about letting go of control of other people. It's hardest with my children because feeling responsible continues to be a habit even though they are grown up now. But I've noticed I have a tendency to want to improve people in general, and to feel I should be able to! Luckily for me, I have a good sense of humor, and now that I understand myself better I can lighten up. When I resent people for their behavior, sometimes it's just because they don't respond to my 'leadership.' I can see the funny side of that, of wanting to be someone's Higher Power. I like myself better when I'm not doing that."

Frozen Feelings

The habit of repressing feelings is a common "protective device" adopted by some of us who live in a painful environment. Frozen feelings make true forgiveness difficult. We may be truly unaware of what we feel. If we have learned to tell ourselves that our feelings are not that important, or if we are ashamed of having a strong emotion, we don't have the tools to begin the forgiveness process. The anger and pain stay with us because, unaware of them, we can't get past them.

Mary Ann's Story: *"I grew up in a family that kept emotions under wraps."*

"I had a difficult marriage when I was young. My late husband's been dead ten years now. I couldn't stop thinking about how he hurt me and all the things he did. At the same time, I tried to convince myself that he wasn't 'that bad,' and maybe I had deserved some of it. Finally, a friend of mine asked me, 'Are you ever going to get over him? Are you going to spend the rest of your life thinking about him?'

"This really got me thinking, so I eventually found a counselor. My counselor helped me understand that I grew up in a family that kept emotions under wraps. I felt I wasn't a good person if I got mad. I felt something was wrong with me if I reacted with feelings.

"I am beginning to know that my feelings count, too, not just other people's. What a relief! I have been seeing my counselor once a week for a year, and now I've developed skills in knowing when I have a reaction to something and not to push it away.

"My goal is to deal with all my feelings about the past and then to be able to forgive my late husband for what happened. I want to forgive myself, too. I already feel more cheerful and positive about my life."

External Reference

Some of us have learned to base our self-esteem on outside factors rather than on our personal accomplishments and preferences. Consequently, we rely on our personal worth being validated by someone else. Another name for this process is being *other-directed*. That is why many people will do anything to hang on to a relationship, even living contrary to their own best interests, since the relationship seems to be such an important part of their identity. This partly explains the undeserved loyalty that we may give to abusive parents or indifferent spouses. It also explains the enormous focus we may have on love and relationships to the exclusion of other important areas such as personal growth or challenging work.

Kevin's Story: *"All I know is that at all costs I wanted everyone to like me."*

"I'd been in A.A. and sober for five years when I became aware that my whole life revolved around impressing or pleasing other people. I know why some people call alcoholics 'charming.' I had to figure out what everyone wanted from me so I would know what to do.

"I know that the positive side of trying so hard to please others is that I have really good intuition about other people's needs. The downside is that I wasn't intuitive about my own needs, which is really ironic. All I know is that at all costs I wanted everyone to like me.

"Now I understand better that I couldn't forgive anyone who hurt me because I didn't really see myself as a separate person who had the right to be treated decently. I had to pretend that everything was okay no matter what. If things got really awful, my only choice as I saw it was to cut the person out of my life. I didn't consider forgiveness and reconciliation as an option. A.A. has been a big help in supporting my efforts to pay attention to Kevin, as well as to stay sober."

When we focus outside ourselves to find our value, we tend to take everything far too personally. If someone we know is an alcoholic, he or she is drinking "against" us. If a friend is in a bad mood, it is sure to be due to something we said or did. The strange thing is, the more reactive we are to the outside world, the more self-centered we are in believing that everyone's behavior leads back to something we imagine we said or did.

Confused Identity

Think of all the people you know who sacrifice their own identities and become "Mrs. Professional Man" or "Mr. Beautiful Young Wife." Think of all the parents you know who feel they own their children's worldly success or failure. Many of us have a difficult time figuring out who is who, or where we stop and someone else begins.

Naturally enough, we become resentful when a spouse or child fails to live up to our expectations and dreams. Often, when others are not at all what we had in mind and behave contrary to our wishes, we may imagine we need to forgive *their* shortcomings. Actually, our high expectations of others can be inappropriate, and what we really need to do is work on strengthening our own identities.

The Fourth Step of Al-Anon can be helpful here: "Made a searching and fearless moral inventory of ourselves."* Part of that process of working the Fourth Step could be to include your dreams, ambitions, wishes, and preferences. When that is done as thoroughly as you can, go back and note which of these dreams are for other people or which of these preferences are for someone else's behavior. Do all of your hopes rest on what other people do with their lives? If that is true, then it is time to pay more attention to yourself.

A good place to begin is to create several short-term and long-term goals for yourself.

· What would you be thinking about if you weren't focused on someone else's life?
· What did you hope to accomplish when you were a child thinking of your future?

---

* All Steps quoted in this article are reprinted with permission of Alcoholics Anonymous World Services, Inc., New York, N.Y., and permission of Al-Anon Family Group Headquarters, Inc. The full Twelve Steps of Alcoholics Anonymous appear in Appendix 1. The full Twelve Steps of Al-Anon appear in Appendix 2.

• List five things that you like to do and figure out a way to do them.

Michelle's Story: *"My husband's life is truly separate from mine."*

"I can remember when I believed that my husband's professional success belonged to me. When his cocaine use led to disaster for his career, I felt personally shamed. My own career was on track, and I had many friends and interests. But somehow I had also incorporated his success into my feelings of worthiness.

"I began my recovery the day I was confronted with what was a new idea to me: my husband's life is truly separate from mine. Only in my emotional 'reality' were his successes and failures mine.

"Though I still care about what happens to him, I don't have to go up and down like a yo-yo as he struggles with his addiction. This enables me to figure out what I really need to forgive him for and what part of my misery is self-inflicted."

Low Self-Esteem

Many of us are familiar with the struggle of feeling bad about how we look, what we accomplish, whether we are caring enough, or whether others approve of us or care for us.

This is a natural result of believing in iron rules about being perfect, being in complete control. Since no one can accomplish these goals, low self-esteem is inevitable. This can lead some of us to believe we don't deserve good things. We may even fail to insist that we be treated decently in a relationship.

If we don't feel worthy of fair treatment in the first place, we may not understand that we have anything to forgive even when someone harms us. Yet, in the daily give-and-take of all relationships, there is frequently a need for forgiveness of the little offenses, if not the big ones.

Joyce Continues: *"I'm beginning to realize that it is hard for me to insist on decent behavior from others."*

Sometimes, when we try to manage other people and fail, our self-esteem falters.

"My Al-Anon sponsor pointed out that since control and trying to manage other people were defects I was working on, I probably had problems with self-esteem too," Joyce says. "It made sense: if I believed I 'should' be able to improve others and had failed, then naturally I would be down on myself.

"I'm beginning to realize that it is hard for me to insist on decent behavior from others. Not that I can change them, but I can change what I do. For example, if my son calls us when he is drinking, I am very firm in ending the call immediately. I tell him I would like to hear from him when he is sober, and then I say good-bye. I act as if I believe I deserve not to listen to abusive talk. And, you know, I am beginning to believe it!"

Caretaking

Taking care of people is a strength. It is terrible to contemplate a world in which we did not take care of each other. But problems arise when the caring is one-sided, or if we are doing for others what they could be doing for themselves, or if others are failing to mature because of our "help." Then caretaking becomes a way of controlling others, and we may feel we have a right to judge and absolve or condemn those whom we caretake.

This kind of caretaker attracts people who don't necessarily want a mutual intimacy, that is, a relationship that nourishes the caretaker as well. *Mutual intimacy* implies an alliance of equals with equal responsibility; caretaking hinders this type of relationship. For both people, caretaking is a one-up, one-down situation in which the "superior" one aids the "needy" one, and there's resentment on both sides.

If the "needy" one resists the control of the caretaker, the caretaker interprets the move as rejection rather than as the healthy bid for growth that it is.

Jason's Story: *"Stan can't be controlled by me."*

"I have a brother who is slowly recovering from marijuana addiction. Stan has always been a worry to our family, and I assumed early the responsibility to explain to him how he should conduct his life. It has been hard sometimes because, though I felt I needed to advise and help Stan, it was never very much appreciated.

"Stan still wears his hair long and shaggy in the old hippie style that I detest. I'm beginning to realize that even when I help him out, Stan can't be controlled by me. In this case, I have to accept that he won't wear his hair to please me.

"The problems between my brother and me won't be resolved if Stan does what I want. Stan needs my support in making his own choices."

Perfectionism

For those of us who are struggling with the need to be perfect and to have others be perfect as well, forgiveness becomes a daily task. *One Day at a Time in Al-Anon* states it well. This trait "makes big problems out of little ones, increases our despair when things don't work out as we hope they will and hampers us in coming to terms with life as it is."

One of the "big problems" is the long list of offenses other have committed against our standards, as well as our own mistakes that we torture ourselves about. We may become consumed as we measure the long list of what we think should not have happened. Or we may become consumed over whether we can forgive ourselves and others "perfectly."

Complicating the issue of forgiveness are the rewards of being unforgiving. It seems strange that suffering estrangement from a loved one or the pain of hating an enemy could bring satisfaction, but they do. One satisfaction is the continued connection with the person, even if only in our own minds, as we replay the wrongs against us. Since a trait of codependency is to dread abandonment—even from abusive people—remembering wrongs can be a form of ongoing connection. Feeling unable to forgive may mean a fear of letting the person go out of our lives, even out of our internal lives.

Another satisfaction of being unforgiving is the power of reproach, especially if the other person is vulnerable to feeling guilty. Collecting resentments over the years can come in handy when we try to get our way with someone who hurt us in the past. Hanging on to past wrongs can be a way of trying to control situations and people.

People can learn to focus on wrongs committed against them, so that they go through life making a collection of their resentments. Consequently, the ability to forgive may require changing our thought patterns or what we tell ourselves about our world.

Sometimes we remind ourselves of others' failures as a way to block out awareness of our own. As Mary Ann, whom we met earlier, noted, "After a few months with my counselor I could hear myself being very unforgiving toward my late husband. This somehow kept me from admitting to myself that I had done some things I'm not proud of. It seems as though if I can learn to forgive myself, then I will be able to forgive him, too."

STAGES OF FORGIVENESS

I believe that forgiveness has five stages.

- Getting Ready
- Hurting
- Hating
- Healing
- Letting Go

Getting Ready

Sometimes it's years after the event until we understand how we've been hurt. This is true for Adult Children of alcoholics, who may connect suddenly with the pain of their childhoods when reading a book on the subject or when working with a counselor. Some childhood traumas may be denied or minimized in adulthood. Jay's father was a compulsive gambler. Gambling was how Jay's father organized his emotional life, how he managed his moods, and how he avoided close contact with his family. Jay was a grown man before he understood how this affected his own life. Today, he describes himself as recovering from codependent behaviors.

Jay's Story: . . . *a 'grown-up' relationship. I like that. I want that for me too."*

"Women tell me I'm too controlling. I know I play Pygmalion, and I have a fantasy of changing a young girl into a perfect woman. I'm attracted to women who seem to need help. I wonder if my dad's behavior has something to do with the fact that I want to be in control and fix people. I used to wish he would stay home, that I could make him different. I plotted for hours, trying to think of something that would make him interested in me.

"I try not to think about my dad, because I never got what I needed from him. I'm in a therapy group now, and I'm beginning to understand that when I'm ready to deal with how I feel about him, it will get me to the point that I can forgive him. I want that, so I can let go. This is still on an intellectual level, but I am hopeful.

"A woman in my group said a really funny thing. She said she used to be attracted to 'wounded birds' instead of men who could give and take in a relationship. Now she's still attracted to them, but she won't act on it. She says that someday she will be ready for a 'grown-up' relationship. I like that. I want that for me too."

Hurting

Spouses of alcoholics or other addicts often take awhile in support groups or counseling "getting ready" for the process of forgiveness. They begin by explaining that they haven't been affected very much by the addiction, or that their main concern is "helping" the addict to stop drinking or using. This is a way to fend off the hurt, although this is the necessary first step to healing.

We become aware that we have been hurt as our denial wears away, and we begin fitting some pieces of painful events together. During this stage, we may be confused for a while before we clearly see how events have affected us.

The First Step of Al-Anon clearly spells out what we need to do: "We admitted we were powerless over alcohol—that our lives had become unmanageable." This Step, admitting how much we have been affected by someone else's addiction, how hurt, frightened, and out of control we feel, is also our first step toward serenity and peace. There is great relief as we stop pretending, as we put ourselves in the hands of our Higher Power, and as we share our pain with others who have "been there" and truly understand.

Anna's Story: *"The hurt I had been putting off for years came at me in waves."*

"I first came to family groups at a treatment center while my husband was in inpatient treatment. I had tried for years to hold my family together and to keep him from drinking too much. As the situation worsened, I survived the traumatic stress by ignoring my feelings as much as I could. I knew that if I fell apart, it would be worse for the children, so I lied to myself and to them about how serious our situation was.

"Since nothing I did kept my husband from drinking, I became more and more depressed and anxious, but like many of us at that stage, my motto seemed to be 'If it doesn't work, do more of it!'

"By the time I showed up in family group, I honestly believed that my only need was for him to stay sober, so I could stop being frightened all the time.

"When I recognized the magnitude of the problem and my contribution to it, the hurt I had been putting off for years came at me in waves. Before I could even consider dealing with my pain and confusion, I needed support from others and education about the family aspects of addiction. Later, I truly understood what 'family recovery' means and, later still, my process of forgiveness began.

"Today, I volunteer at that same treatment center, greeting new families to the program. I'm very gentle with them, because I remember when I, too, believed the only important thing was that the alcoholic in the family got sober."

*   *   *

Many of us learn to say, ''I know it's a disease now, so of course I forgive.'' But true forgiveness of oneself and the addict is a later stage, when our understanding has deepened and our feelings have been acknowledged and processed.

Hating

This is the blaming, angry stage when we see the other person as totally responsible for the terrible way we feel. We feel powerless and helpless. Since we can't change the past or the other person, it truly feels as though we're trapped and can change nothing.

Janis's Story: *"I felt that losing my husband was a death of a large part of myself."*

''After twenty years of marriage, my husband wanted a divorce to marry someone else. He said he still had feelings for me as well as a strong feeling of guilt, but he was convinced that his happiness depended on being with the other woman. No matter how I explained to him that he was just in a mid-life crisis, he was determined to go through with his plans.

''I was hurt and scared because I loved him. I know I draw most of my identity from my connections with other people, but that is the way most women of my generation were brought up. I felt that losing my husband was a death of a large part of myself.

''Since I tried to control others to get what I wanted, my efforts to manage him and his behavior only alienated him further. I shifted into trying to 'help' him adjust to our divorce by recommending different counselors and divorce support groups. These tactics all failed and left me feeling ashamed and terrible about myself.''

Janis is recovering from the loss of her husband. She is beginning to understand how codependency made the loss even harder to bear. She now wonders how much of her love for him was good for either of them. Divorce was traumatic for her, but it was a catalyst for her growth.

She identifies her forgiveness process as still being in the hating stage. She fantasizes about his remorse, hopes the other woman hurts him, and complains about him to all her friends. He is still very much on her mind most of the time. As she focuses on her recovery and puts more meaning into her life, in time she will realize she is finally into the next phase of forgiveness: healing.

Being angry at or hating ourselves can complicate forgiveness as much as being angry at others. As we become aware of how we contributed to events that hurt us so much, it is very difficult to forgive ourselves. We may experience a sort of internal civil war if we blame ourselves and focus on regrets.

Sometimes we may have contributed to our problems. Other times, we truly have been victimized, but we blame ourselves unreasonably. It's a good idea to sort this out with a counselor, since someone else's perspective can strengthen our insights. Discussing our anger is useful because if we are contributing to our pain, we need to know that in order to get our lives straightened out. If we are not contributing to our pain, then we still need to understand if and how we are being unfair to ourselves.

Healing

One of the most serious blocks to forgiveness is today's pain that reminds us of pain in the past. The past can haunt us and make us very reactive to present problems. We may even feel as though we're being assaulted all over again, unless we begin trying to resolve the hurts from the past that still influence our feelings and attitudes.

Bob's Story: *"Now my second marriage threatens to go under at times. . . ."*

"I was married for twenty-five years to my first wife, who suffered from serious depression. She attempted suicide several times, was hysterical almost daily, and abused me verbally when I gave up trying to talk to her.

"Now my second marriage threatens to go under at times because I feel overwhelmingly anxious if my new wife gets moody. For me, any deviation from what I perceive as 'normal' is a possible recurrence of what I went through before. This makes it difficult to let go of a behavior that another person might consider merely annoying. Our marriage counselor is helping me to sort out what belongs to this marriage for me and what is still unhealed from my first marriage. It has really helped to understand why I react the way I do."

Sandi's Story: *"I developed a complete fantasy about taking them [my parents] to court for 'malpractice.'"*

Forgiving the past is even more complicated if the same people who hurt us in the past are involved with today's difficulties.

"I have two alcoholic parents," Sandi says. "There was plenty of money for the family to spend when I was growing up, and I got many advantages. I had dancing lessons, expensive clothes, and any material thing I wanted. But I had no healthy model for relationships. My parents freely insulted each other, and no one ever focused on my emotional needs.

"I struggle today with letting go of that past and forgiving my parents. I try to fill in the gaps they left with counseling, belonging to a Twelve Step program, and seeking out emotionally healthy older women as mentors and sponsors.

"Forgiveness is made more difficult because my parents are still incapable of a good relationship with me. And contact with them usually leaves me feeling the pain of the past as well as the pain of the present.

"While searching for a way to release my feelings about them, I developed a complete fantasy about taking them to court for 'malpractice.' Since they have so much respect in our town, outsiders would never guess at my childhood. I imagine witnesses and a brilliant prosecuting attorney who publicly exposes what they did, while giving my two sisters and me the affirmation and support we never had.

"This fantasy gives my anger a focus and makes me feel better. I notice I am gradually thinking about it less as my real life improves. My goal is to accept them today for what they are and are not, because I know I can have a good life even if they never change. That is what my program has done for me.''

The healing stage is a working stage. Both Bob and Sandi actively participate in a conscious forgiveness process. Bob is in marriage counseling, and Sandi is in support groups as well as in therapy.

Letting Go

The final stage of forgiving ourselves and others is letting go. This is the hardest stage to describe since it doesn't have as many obvious outward signs.

Letting go is an internal event for us. Others will probably notice it only by the absence of our former behavior, such as our once familiar discussions of suffering, or our once frequent attempts to control. For me, this stage is perfectly expressed by the Serenity Prayer:

> *God grant me the serenity*
> *To accept the things I cannot change,*
> *The courage to change the things I can,*
> *And the wisdom to know the difference.*

I can't change the past or the way other people do things. I am peaceful when I accept that.

The letting go stage may include welcoming the people with whom we were codependent back into our lives or our trust. This depends as much on the other person as it does on us. Can that person act differently today and understand how we were hurt? Is it likely we can begin another phase of our relationship, based on a willingness to act differently?

Letting go is detachment from distress. We no longer feel driven to do something about the person who hurt us, or about our reactions. Sometimes the painful event loses all its importance for us. Or we may become aware that because of what happened we took a different road that led to a very satisfying destination. As we let go, we discover that we go days, then weeks, then months without thinking about what happened that was so painful.

GETTING THERE

Successful forgiveness can be a confusing struggle, because forgiveness doesn't come naturally to many of us who are confronting codependency issues. Forgiveness must be consciously nurtured. But it can become easier with practice.

Some special problems may complicate the process.

- The "Unforgivable"
- Ongoing Anger
- Preferences Versus Demands
- Repetitive Memories
- Self-Forgiveness
- "I Want to, But I Can't"

The "Unforgivable"

For many people, it makes sense to label some things in the past as unforgivable, such as abuse of children. They believe that to forgive is to excuse. But in recovery, many people have discovered that it is even possible to let go of these unforgivables.

Some people visualize letting go of an unforgivable past as giving the past over to the care of their Higher Power. If the present relationship with a person is good but the past interferes, it can help to visualize boundaries around the past in order to preserve what is good today. If the relationship has never been something worth preserving, or the unforgivable act was committed by a stranger, the painful experiences can still be segregated and the pain can be "turned over." This does not excuse what happened, but makes it possible for us to let go.

The Third Step of Al-Anon is: "Made a decision to turn our will and our lives over to the care of God *as we understood Him*." However we understand a Higher Power in our lives, the unforgivable can be released from our hearts in this way.

Ongoing Anger

We may doubt we have forgiven if we can still get angry about the past, even if we no longer feel hatred for the person or people associated with our pain. It's natural enough not to feel placid about past suffering, even if it no longer occupies our daily thoughts.

Or we may feel forgiveness is impossible because the same behavior is still going on; for example, the affairs, the violence, or the indifference to our needs continue.

We may need to take action, as in the case of a family member who is chemically dependent; this may include treatment or separation. But forgiveness has the potential of enabling abuse. Be sure that forgiveness is not misused as an excuse to allow harmful behavior to continue. Be sure, too, that forgiveness is healing for all parties and allows healthy decisions to be made.

Each time we remember that we have healthy options, aside from endless reacting, and *act on that belief*, we are stronger and feel more in control of our lives. We can list our abilities or our choices that have been taken from us and decide how we are going to exercise our options and get back our power. Pause a moment now and answer these questions:

- If you are an Adult Child from a family where there was a lot of pain and you were denied a chance to play or were criticized when you were joyful or loud, what can you do now to take loving care of yourself?
- What are the playful things you would enjoy doing?
- If you are the spouse of an addicted person, are you living with put-downs that erode your self-esteem?
- What activities make you feel better about yourself?
- Are you in a support group that helps you detach emotionally from the abusive person's behavior?

Healing occurs as we take care of ourselves as our "best revenge" against the people who hurt us.

It helps if we discuss thoroughly our angry feelings with a trusted sponsor, friend, or counselor. We can also write down what happened to us and how we reacted. This helps to validate that the events really happened and that we have a right to have feelings about them. This doesn't come naturally to many of us, but we need to keep this in mind.

As Kevin shared in an earlier example, we may be so eager to please others that we forget our right to fair treatment in a relationship. Or our self-esteem may be so battered that we will "forgive" everything and allow ourselves to be further abused.

Preferences Versus Demands

Think about the difference between our preferences and our demands. We may prefer that someone be quiet and studious rather than active and demanding, but to attempt to demand a change in character would be a disaster. We can learn to forgive people for what they do, not for their failure to be who we prefer them to be.

A careful overview of ourselves can also include the Fifth Step of Al-Anon: "Admitted to God, to ourselves and to another human being the exact nature of our wrongs." Working Step Five can expose our self-centered resentment against people for being who they are and not who we want them to be. We can forgive wrongs against ourselves, but nobody has the right to demand that someone else be a different person.

Repetitive Memories

When we have been wronged and we recognize it, it's natural to think about the events frequently. The thoughts may intrude again and again, even when we wish they wouldn't. Eventually, we recognize that we're punishing ourselves with painful memories and we're reliving the pain. That may be the point where we decide we need to free ourselves by forgiveness.

Michael has discovered that meditation or prayer has helped in his process of forgiving his wife for her use of cocaine. "It helps me to live in the present and to detach from the past. I pray for her peace as well as my own and I leave my wife to her Higher Power for whatever lessons are necessary."

Some people with codependent tendencies believe that part of their role in relationships is to teach others how to improve their lives. Michael has decided that this is not in his "husbandly job description," and he and his wife will both be better off if she learns from *her* experiences rather than from his expectations.

Self-Forgiveness

Many of us feel that forgiving ourselves is the hardest task of all. Anna admits to this, adding, "I know in my head that I did the best I could with a very hard situation, but in my heart I still wish I had handled the situation differently, with the children particularly. Part of my dedication to my volunteer work at the treatment center is a 'penance' I assigned myself.

"That may sound strange to some people, but when I don't feel like going, I tell myself it's my way to make up for what I didn't do well. Helping others heal is part of my way of making amends. Of course, our family is much healthier today because we handle things differently, but I still feel a need to make up for the past. Since I figured out a way to do this that works for me, I have felt much better, more forgiving of myself. I believe this method could work for many people: finding a creative way to do good and heal the pain of self-blame at the same time."

Step Eight of Alcoholics Anonymous and Al-Anon is: "Made a list of all persons we had harmed, and became willing to make amends to them all." Making amends helps us to forgive ourselves, but only when we do this with sensitivity toward those to whom we need to make amends. Asking for forgiveness only so *we* can feel better is just more of the same self-centeredness. But asking how we can help to heal the past can help us move toward forgiving ourselves and others.

Some of us can find relief from self-blame by concentrating on how differently we handle things today. Today can be a better yesterday. And, eventually, we'll have many more good yesterdays than sad ones.

I Want To, But I Can't

Our motives and feelings are often obscure to us. Exploration of them can bring surprising results. If forgiveness seems impossible, some therapists suggest that we write down what is unforgivable and follow it with "I can't (won't) forgive because _____." For example, I can't (won't) forgive because

- I will have to take care of myself.
- I will have to face loneliness.
- I will lose control of the situation.
- I will lose the person forever.
- I will lose my one-up position.
- I will have to forgive myself, too, and I don't know how.
- I will have to deal with that person again.
- I will have to deal with the situation again.

Then complete this sentence: The advantages to having resentments are _____. For example, the advantages to having resentments are:

• they justify what I do; otherwise, I would feel I was wrong.
• they keep me from seeing the emptiness in my life.
• they give me an excuse for failing to achieve.

Janis admitted that she spent much more money on her wardrobe than the family could afford, but she dealt with her guilt about it by reminding herself of her husband's infidelity.

Another possibility is that not forgiving enables us to make excuses for not achieving what we think we should have achieved. We may say to ourselves that because of our alcoholic parents, or impossible spouses, or problem children, we have been held back from fulfilling our true potential. Whatever our reasons are, they keep us prisoners of pain, and they reveal codependent traits as well; a need to control, fear of abandonment, and the belief that we don't have power of choice in our lives. At some level, we may fear the emptiness that will be there if we give up resentment and hurt. These feelings are taking up room, so to speak. They have a life of their own; they are an emotional reality. It's to our advantage to understand our emotional logic.

Janis Continues: *"I definitely need a new life of my own. . . ."*

Janis has come to believe that some of what she needs to do to forgive her ex-husband involves understanding herself better.

"Forgiving him means letting go of him. In recovery, I've come to see how mistaken I was to believe that I could hang on to him by hanging on to my anger. It was as if there would be an empty space in my heart if I stopped reacting to him and his behavior. I couldn't seem to imagine ever filling that space with more positive thoughts. Now I see that this 'logic' didn't really make sense. I now see how I used resentment as a connection to him, which hurt me more than him. I definitely need a new life of my own, and I'm working on it."

Kevin Continues: *"Forgiveness happens when I don't give people the power to hurt me."*

Kevin also recognizes the extent to which his thinking gives him problems. "I control my serenity by what I think and what I do. If dwelling on what other people do gets me upset, then meetings and reading recovery literature help. I choose to do what works for me. I don't push away my feelings anymore; I examine them. Forgiveness happens when I don't give people the power to hurt me.

"We all have the power to create a better life this way, by discovering our power to change. It's been good for my self-esteem to give myself credit for these efforts. Other people have helped, but I've worked hard at it too. Those of us who have this new life have found it by accepting powerlessness over alcohol, other drugs, and other people. This is how we've found the personal power to change and grow. Good times are not just for other people; they're for me too!''

Anna Continues: *"I've learned that I have some very good instincts for taking care of myself."*

Feeling her pain, and resolving it, has helped Anna in the healing process. "Believe it or not, for me pain has been a blessing," she says. "It told me what was going on when I didn't want to know. Just as I've learned to listen to my feelings, I've learned that I have some very good instincts for taking care of myself. The key is to settle down and not jump to wild conclusions. Sometimes, something will set me off or trigger me into anger about the bad old days. The difference is now I know what I can do about it.

"For one thing, I practice my 'attitude of gratitude.' That is a cliché just because so many people have discovered that it works. I keep in touch with all the blessings in my life, including the pain that has helped me to heal, but also the many pleasures and gifts in each day. I concentrate on them; I keep aware of them.

"Sometimes I also 'act as if' I am the loving, stable human being I wish I were all the time. It can get me past times when I feel cranky and could easily say or do something hurtful to someone else.

"Something else that works for me in getting to forgiveness is some insight into why a person may behave a certain way. It doesn't mean that it was all right that I got hurt. It's not healthy for me to believe my feelings aren't important. But it helps to give some thought as to how and why the other person behaves in a certain way.

"My mother is difficult for me to be with at times,

for example. She can be demanding that things go her way, and she remembers every slight she ever received. I had heard the story many times about her childhood, how uncaring her father was, the feeling she had that no one was behind her. I mentioned the problems I was having with her at a meeting, and someone said, 'She sure sounds like an Adult Child to me!'

"Well, I know that not all children of alcoholics are just like that, but it rang a bell with me. I began to think of all the behavior I reacted to, and I put it into a framework of her childhood. Now I feel much better about her; I don't take it so personally. I think of that little girl inside her that is still so hurt, and I love her instead of resenting her. The truth is, we have always had lots of good times together too."

Joyce Continues: *"I know what to do to keep my attitudes healthy."*

People with experience in practicing forgiveness have tips to share with each other. Joyce suggests that for her there are warning signs of slipping into a resentful attitude.

"If I get too busy for comfort, or get careless about my health routines, which for me is eating lightly and an exercise program, then I am tired and have poorer self-esteem. As a result, I set myself up for being too reactive to what others say and do. I know what to do to keep my attitudes healthy.

"I have also learned to recognize how I feel on the brink of a slip into an unforgiving or critical state. I grew up in a home that gave a high moral value to being busy and taking responsibility for other people's behavior. So I can get on a roll of ignoring my need for leisure as well as assuming control over the uncontrollable. Eventually, I am upset and angry with everyone.

"I can nip all that in the bud by changing what I'm doing before it's a full-blown situation. It was good to learn that I can have a positive effect on my own moods. I am active in Al-Anon, and we have a program that recommends frequent attention to our own thoughts and actions.

"Step Ten says, 'Continued to take personal inventory and when we were wrong promptly admitted it.' I take my inventory every day, and I often don't even have anything to admit because I'm able to check myself before setting on a wrong course.

"This actually means I have less to forgive others for too. I don't have as many unreasonable expectations for other people, and I don't provoke as much anger in them as I used to either."

GIFTS OF FORGIVENESS

Forgiveness, the practice of letting go of grudges and resentments, brings the gifts of self-respect and personal power. It is part of a spiritual path, by which I mean acknowledging that there is a Power greater than ourselves and that we are only a small part of the whole. Forgiveness is also, for me, a commitment to not harming others, a willingness to be tolerant and gentle.

This commitment to not harming others is extended

to ourselves as well. We will need to forgive others and ourselves all our lives, but that does not mean we should tolerate mistreatment and enable it to continue unchallenged.

Without recovery, addicts and other compulsive people continue to repeat the behaviors that hurt those who love them. And even with recovery, sometimes the painful events come so fast that there is no time to catch our breath and even think about forgiveness. We may need to put certain people out of our lives. Certainly, we need to practice detachment, if not from the person, then at least from our painful involvement.

Why Codependency Is a Useful Concept

Codependency describes a condition in which our need for control, our fears of abandonment, and our tendency to take care of everyone but ourselves can destroy our chances for happiness. Yet there is hope that as we understand our behavior patterns learned in childhood, we can deliberately act differently until we have developed new, healthy behavior. We can lean on the wisdom of others as we explore our feelings and begin to treat ourselves with respect.

As we become less controlling, less frightened of losing loved ones, and less at odds with ourselves, we become more loving and more forgiving of everyone in our lives. As we focus less on changing others, we become more tolerant of their shortcomings. As we work on what Al-Anon and Alcoholics Anonymous call "character defects" (what many therapists now call "codependency traits"), we find that forgiveness becomes easier and easier.

Forgiveness gives us personal power that we never had when we tried to have power over others. It frees us to do the work we were meant to do. And sometimes, it gives us a way to love someone without pain.

WHEN HUMOR HURTS

Roseann Lloyd

Laughter can be a wonderful part of life. A good joke can lift our spirits when we're down. A humorous observation may turn the mood of a day from pessimistic to optimistic. A good belly laugh may help us let go of worrying about our immediate problems. Sometimes humor literally lifts our physical body to a more joyous state.

But humor also has its downside. Sometimes laughter is a way for us to avoid expressing pain. At other times, we laugh, nervously, to avoid conflict. Some of us laugh to keep our life floating on the surface, to keep the party moving. Sometimes our frustration or anger is expressed through jokes that disparage other people. This kind of humor is very destructive. It hurts others as well as ourselves. Sarcasm, after all, comes from words that mean *to tear flesh*.

In this chapter, we'll examine humor and consider the benefits of changing our sense of humor. Changing it doesn't mean losing it. I'm writing from my own experience and from that of people close to me who have also struggled with this issue. As I've changed, my relationships have changed, and humor has been a topic that has been talked about.

I grew up in a family that prized a good sense of humor. Everybody was good at kidding around. Being a smart aleck went with the territory. There wasn't just one family clown—all of us kids were good at the quick comeback and smart remark. Many of the family stories that go back several generations have a humorous turn to them.

But there was also tension in the humor. If you cried when you got teased, the teasing escalated. One of my first memories is the day I tried to learn to roller skate. The sidewalk in front of our house was made out of bricks. I cried in frustration when I fell down and cried even harder when I noticed that my uncle was laughing at me and recording my anguish on his home-movie camera.

Now as an adult, I remember such episodes and see that teasing and a sarcastic give-and-take were typical forms of communication. We hardly ever said anything directly. Our family wasn't unique—I see indirect communication in many families and other places in our culture. The large number of words that are synonyms for sarcasm is an indication of how prevalent it is as a form of communication:

- the quick comeback
- the indirect compliment
- clever repartee—"touché!"
- irony
- sharp tongue
- the zinger that goes through the room as you walk out the door

- back talk
- the put-down
- the witty retort
- "damned by faint praise"
- amusing commentary

Teenagers have their own words for this: "You really dogged him." "You dis-ed her. . . ."

What I didn't realize when I was a kid was that being a smart aleck was a survival tool. It was how we lived. I didn't know anything about direct communication of ideas and feelings. I didn't know that it was possible to express feelings—especially affection and anger and frustration—in any other way than an indirect way.

This heritage of humor is both a gift and a burden. We see that laughter can be a source of pleasure and relaxation. But it can also have a harmful effect on us and our relationships because it sometimes blocks intimacy, blocks the direct expression of feelings, thoughts, and ideas. Humor is not always in our best interest. We have to learn when to let go of it.

Healthy Humor—We Could All Use a Good Laugh

Laughing can be joyful. It's part of good mental health. As a standard of excellence for humor, I think the best jokes, books, or comedies are those that can get me to laugh out loud, even when I'm alone.

Laughter can make the difference between a blah day and a day that we feel is filled with energy and joy. Think of all the sayings that are trite but somehow indicate this truth:

- "Walk on the sunny side of the street."
- "Look on the bright side of things."
- "Is the glass of water half full or half empty?"

The truth of these sayings is that laughter can help us live in the present moment. When we laugh, we forget the pain of the past, and we let go of worry about the future.

When we're in a group, laughter can bring us together. It gives us closeness and bonding. Jean Illsley Clarke and Connie Dawson, in their book *Growing Up Again: Parenting Ourselves, Parenting Our Children*, offer an excellent discussion of humor.

> *Joyous laughter at a joke that disparages no one, or laughing in an empathetic way, builds esteem and offers intimacy. It invites people to feel special and signals that they are "insiders." As an example: Charlie brought flowers to his wife for her birthday, not realizing he was one week early. Ginny and the children genuinely enjoyed the surprise of his "mistake," and he joined in the laughter.*

Laughter also has a quality of healing. Norman Cousins is famous for writing about this quality in *Anatomy of an Illness*. He tells about discovering that he had a serious illness and deciding to cure himself by renting old movies and laughing every day.

I think he's on to something. When I was recovering from surgery a few years ago, I decided to write one funny paragraph every day to help my recovery. I don't know whether I really got better faster than I would have otherwise, but I enjoyed my time being an invalid. In fact, my memory of that time of my life is much more peaceful than many others.

Laughter as a good thing seems even more important as we get older. Besides the possibility of illness, we face the mid-life disappointments and normal aches and pains. I was somewhat startled to realize recently that comedies are the only kind of movies I attend these days. I remember being a teenager and being disgusted with middle-aged people who didn't want to go to Ingmar Bergman movies because he was too "depressing." Now I hear myself talking the way they did: "I don't want to have any more of that angst in my life. I've had enough excitement. If I'm going to spend an evening out, I want to be *entertained*." You know you're middle-aged when you start going to comedies.

We're So Hungry for Humor

We can see evidence that people hunger for humor when we look at the personals ads in some newspapers. One of the first qualities people specify is that they want to go out with someone "with a good sense of humor." Not many want to admit they don't have a good sense of humor.

How can we bring more humor into our lives other than advertising in the personals? It's worth taking some

time to think about. I like to write funny postcards to
my friends. I like to rent old Pink Panther movies. I like
to laugh over nothing. Finding opportunities for laughter is as important as planning for physical exercise or
eating good food.

But when does humor turn on itself?

Cheerfulness—Humor Turned into Caretaking

Humor smooths the wheels of social interaction. It
keeps things moving along. Humor can brighten the
mood of a group. It can help a group become unified
and experience bonding through a shared experience. It
can lighten the quiet sadness and break through the
tension produced by conflict and anger. Humor also
makes the humdrum interesting; it adds spice to an
ordinary conversation. Humor escalates the intensity of
a good mood.

If we are good at making jokes and "oiling the
wheels of interaction," we may feel responsible to keep
the group moving along in a way that is not healthy for
us. We may feel over-responsible. Whenever we use
humor for the sake of the group at the expense of our
own needs, we're actually caretaking or engaging in
other codependent behavior. I define codependency as
*behavior that shows more concern for the needs of oth-
ers than our own—to the extent that we are being
harmed*.

One way to find out how much our culture expects us
to be cheery is to walk around looking serious for a
couple of days. I've heard people talk about being verbally accosted in public by strangers for not being
cheerful. Both women and men report the cultural pres-

sures to be *up and at 'em*. Being responsible for a constant upbeat mood creates its own kind of tension. We all need our down time.

A few years ago, after I stopped thinking I had to be "up" and pleasant all the time, my family thought something was wrong with me. My daughter looked at me, asking, "Are you mad?"

"Nothing is wrong," I said. "This is me; this is how my face looks when I'm being quiet. You have to trust me to tell you if there is anything wrong."

One of my lifelong friends said, "Your face in repose is rather somber." I looked in the mirror. You know, she was right. My face was scary looking to me—it was unfamiliar. But I practiced thinking, *It's okay to look somber, if that's really me*.

I also have a joyful side that is "really me": on my desk is a picture of me, age three, with a natural joyfulness, which is not to be confused with fake cheeriness. I get to feel the way I feel, and it's not the same every day.

Humor as a Defense Mechanism

In the process of working on my own sense of humor, I've discovered that humor is my best defense mechanism. You may ask, what does a defense mechanism do? It protects us. I think of a defense mechanism as a big roll of cotton that I use to wrap around me to make the world less harsh. In relationships, a defense mechanism protects us from feeling our feelings, and feeling the pain of other people's feelings.

I decided to use my journal and, for a few days, record every event that prompted me to joke around.

During that time, I refrained from joking. I did it for about three days. My journal was thick with examples. I didn't like the exercise. Whenever I wanted to crack jokes and refrained from doing so, I felt deprived, bereft, fearful, and powerless. I felt "less than" when I couldn't smooth things over with a joke. I also felt that I lost some personal power. I had that famous feeling called *loss of control.* I had these feelings at the same time, an indication to me of the power of what I was giving up.

I also felt like I was letting other people down. I wasn't doing what was expected of me; I wasn't entertaining the group. Then it dawned on me that maybe people weren't expecting to be entertained. Did I ask people if they expected me to do this? Well, no, I hadn't, but I did have the past experience at being appreciated for being funny. I decided to continue working on this and not being "up" every day. As time has passed, I've become more at ease with not being funny. I still feel "less than," but I live with the discomfort. When I'm not being funny, other feelings come in.

Most of us enjoy laughing—healthy laughing. But we want to be free of compulsive joke-telling and people-pleasing humor. We want to choose when to let ourselves be funny.

Humor Blocks Out Other Feelings

Whenever I use humor to soften the rough edges, I need to stop and see if I'm shutting out other feelings that may need to be expressed.

At one time there were some things I had done that had hurt my daughter, and even though I thought I'd acknowledged that she'd been hurt, she didn't feel heard. She didn't think I had apologized. I wanted to move on, lighten up. Finally I understood that I needed to sit still, listen, and acknowledge her pain before we could move on. I had known about her pain, but I didn't want to sit still and let it be in the room with us.

I call this kind of behavior "playing Mary Poppins" in the family: I lacked the ability to say, "I know you're hurting. I'm really sorry that this hurt you."

Playing the role of Mary Poppins also means that it's hard for me to say that anything hurts me. I am learning now how to do this. There is a great freedom in being able to say, "That hurt."

After working on this issue for several years, I see that my sense of humor blocked the free expression of feelings in many areas in my life. Being able to listen to pain, and express pain, was the primary step in recovering my feelings. Other feelings that are now more present in my life are more intimacy, more affection, more relaxation. Negative feelings like anger, sorrow, and loneliness are expressed more directly and processed faster. There is more of a flow in my emotional life than there was before. Although my concern about humor began with its role in my relationships, the change has also affected my work and writing. As I change, I have been able to state my opinions more directly in my writing.

Gallows Humor Distracts Us from Our Pain

Discounting pain is not healthy. I've always been good at joking during times of stress. Laughing at pain can work as destructive caretaking and discounting our essential self. Some people call this *gallows humor*. The expression *gallows humor* comes from the custom of requiring a person on the gallows to tell a joke right before he is hung so that the crowd will laugh at the hanging. The joke distracts the crowd from the actual death they are witnessing. So the term *gallows humor* is powerful in reminding us that jokes distract. Some people, especially in literary circles, use the term *black humor*. I am opposed to the use of the term, for it is racist in that it links the word *black* with painful experiences. It gives a negative connotation to the word *black*. *Gallows humor* is apt and useable.

Using gallows humor distracts us from pain. It can work so well that we can be in situations that are endangering us and we don't know it. In this way, what we're calling "a defense mechanism" is the same as denial. If we are in a dangerous situation and laugh about it, we are denying its seriousness and the possibility we are being hurt. We're not letting ourselves feel fear, anger, sorrow—any number of powerful negative feelings. Fear and anger are often called "negative emotions," but they also protect us because they tell us when we're in danger.

A friend of mine said:

> *I came into treatment with my neck and my hand in a cast. And yet, when I was asked in group, I couldn't think of any negative consequences I had experienced from my drinking. I had to learn to stop laughing. I think that was the hardest part of treatment. Laughing was all I had left. It was harder to give up than drinking.*

From this story, we see that it may be so painful to give up humor that we feel that we are giving up our soul. This story may remind us of one from our own life.

We may stop for a minute now and think about what we might gain by changing our sense of humor: more moments of closeness with people we care about, a deeper sense of who we are, a greater awareness of dangerous situations, and the possibility of recovery.

Sometimes movies can help us see our own behavior and our personal history. I loved the movie *The Great Santini*. In it, the power of the abusive, cruel father is held at bay by the oldest girl's back talk, sarcasm, and off-the-wall, hilarious commentaries on life. In this child, I saw the brave attempt to try to control a crazy situation through humor. I felt myself sending her love for her bravery and yet wanting to tell her: "Stop, it will never work. Just get out of there!" I felt full of sorrow for this child who was giving such incredible energy to a situation that she didn't have the power to change.

We are adults now, and we can learn to recognize our own pain and recognize when we are in danger. Once we know the meaning of the word *safe*, and how it feels to be safe, we will learn to recognize other feelings as well.

I Laughed Until I Cried

I've often heard people say with a great sense of relief: "Oh, I laughed until I cried." It sounds like sometimes the only way we can get to our tears is through laughing, that we work through to our pain through laughing. This is telling us that we do indeed need to get to our tears.

If we learned in childhood not to cry, not to admit pain, then we need to unlearn that now. Learning to cry, I think, is one of the tasks of growing up, of becoming a mature person. It has taken me a long time to learn to cry. When I first got the tears flowing, it was scary because it felt like the tears came from a bottomless pit—that I'd never stop. Now I can see that the crying comes and goes. I figure that if I spent forty years not crying, I have a lot of lost time to make up for. It may take me another twenty-five years to get the sorrow and joy in balance, but it's a great relief to not have to hold back those tears anymore.

The Person Telling the Jokes
Is the One with the Upper Hand

Humor, in addition to being a powerful defense mechanism, is a method for staying in control of situations. I didn't understand the connection between humor and control until I gave up my old sense of humor, because as I let go of it I felt powerless. I learned what it was as I lost it.

Like many other methods of control, something that looks weak is powerful, and something powerful may appear to be weak. When I'm being cheery and humorous, it looks like I'm serving the group (the family, the meeting, the class, etc.), and in some cases that is true. But it is also true that as long as the jokes keep coming, nobody else can get in there and say anything serious. Being funny and cheerful is a sneaky way of controlling a situation; I get to be in control and look like I'm not.

What is control? Whenever we're trying to be in control, we don't want to feel our own feelings. We don't want to let in other people's feelings. We're also trying to control others' impressions of us—wanting to be seen as not weak, not a victim. When we're trying to be in control, we're also controlling the atmosphere: making the room predictable. Whenever we're trying to be in control, we're not having much trust in the world and in other people. We may be reacting to childhood, where the world was not trustworthy, where the people were out of control. And it's important to say here, again, that humor gives the illusion of control because it never directly deals with the situation at hand.

I figure that I learned this lighthearted, smart-aleck behavior in my childhood, and I needed to have it then. The hardest part of giving it up is getting used to the silence, the uneasiness when I'm not jumping in to talk. It's not that life is out of control; it's just that I don't want the emptiness that I feel when I think I have control of the situation, which was, all along, an illusion anyway.

Like my friends who are also changing their senses of humor, I've gradually learned to give up certain kinds of humor, in certain situations, such as compulsive humor, caretaking humor, or sarcasm. I think that I've been able to do this because I've learned to have more trust in the world and in those I love, and more trust in myself to handle life without the constant wisecrack. Directly stating my feelings is not as scary as it used to be. Solving problems is not as scary as it used to be. Silence is not as scary as it used to be.

And now when life is funny, it's really funny, in a gentle, noncompulsive way.

When Humor Gets Out of Hand: Teasing, Ridicule, and Sarcasm

We've seen that even "good" humor can be used in destructive ways when we are trying to control a situation or avoid feelings. But "bad" humor is almost always bad because it is destructive to the people it's used on.

There are many synonyms for bad humor:

- teasing
- making fun of
- ridiculing
- put-downs
- insulting
- irony
- belittling
- holding in contempt
- name-calling
- sarcasm

As mentioned earlier, *sarcasm* came from words meaning *to tear the flesh*. I think of these words as applying to all forms of humor that tear down other people. Although some people have said that sarcasm is sideways anger, I think that expression is too mild. Sarcasm is more than anger; it's hostility, for its function is to diminish another person. It is hostile and shaming. It can come out of quite legitimate frustration, anger, and pain, but it is expressed as hostility toward another person.

When I think about humor that hurts other people, I also think of situations in which some people tell jokes that put down and humiliate other people—jokes that are racist, sexist, or sexually offensive, jokes about disabled or retarded people. Sometimes it seems that the joke tellers are telling the joke in order to embarrass the listeners as well. The joke dares listeners to comment on the joke teller's hostility. The joke becomes a challenge and a statement of power. The humor is being used as a way to assert control over a situation. It really has nothing to do with being funny. It has nothing to do with the gift of joyful humor that bonds a group and brings sharing.

Hostile humor was very much a part of my upbringing and much of my adult life. I think of it as the American way of life: to see how much you can exchange insults and not show that you're hurt. Many of us have probably gotten up the courage to say that a remark hurt, only to find the other person saying, "I was only joking," or, "Don't you have a sense of humor?"

The Sarcasm Recovery Chronicles

When I began realizing how destructive this kind of humor is, I started to work on changing some of my behavior. I realized that there were certain situations I couldn't be a part of: for example, playing competitive games like bridge brought out all my sarcastic remarks. I had to stop playing card games. I couldn't handle myself.

Later I realized how much the kind of party banter that passes for humor was based on put-downs of other people. I shudder when I remember some of the things a friend, Colleen, and I said about our musician husbands—that we were going to take all their Martin guitars and antique mandolins and put them in a trash compactor and rewrap them as matchbox toys. To tell you the truth, that still sounds pretty funny to me, but what I feel now is the pain—our feelings of loneliness and of being left out, and the pain the guys must have felt when we laughed at them in public.

As I've continued to work on this issue, I've discovered that my smart-aleck behavior affected my early behavior as a parent. Only recently have I realized the extent of harm that sarcasm brings to children. When my daughter was a baby, I thought that I was being loving and affirming, and in many ways I was. I didn't consciously use put-downs, name-calling, ridiculing, and teasing. (On the contrary, I consciously worked on being affirming.) But some ridiculing came out anyway, because I wasn't conscious of how much it was part of me. She has told me that one of her earliest memories is of walking down the hallway of her dad's office and being mad. She doesn't remember what she was mad about, but she remembers that both of us were teasing her and calling her "Fat Lip." It breaks my heart when I think of this story. I have no memory of the event. I have no doubt that it is true. It affected her self-confidence.

I have made drastic changes in my life. One of the most important was giving up sarcasm forever.

Eventually I decided to go cold turkey on all put-downs, name-calling, ridiculing, and teasing. It was too painful for me to figure out when it was okay and when it wasn't. Now I'm unsure of how to do kidding in a loving way. I don't even try to fake it. That's one of the holes I can live with.

Unilateral Disarmament

A pamphlet that is very useful for giving up sarcasm is *I Deserve Respect: Finding and Healing Shame in Personal Relationships* by Ronald and Patricia Potter-Efron.* They suggest that we make a decision to give up all put-downs and shaming behaviors, regardless of what other people do. They outline a plan for unilateral disarmament:

> *The point is that we can't wait for the world to become a nice place. We can't wait until everybody else quits shaming us before we make a serious commitment to change our behavior. Self-determination means we are responsible for our own behavior. The time to stop shaming the people we care about is as soon as we realize that belittling them only diminishes ourselves.*

Another useful book for parents who want to give up sarcasm is *Growing Up Again* by Jean Illsley Clarke and Connie Dawson.* It is a great resource for changing our behavior as parents. In this book, the destructive power of teasing, ridiculing, and sarcasm is discussed, and ways to change are offered.

If we have been in relationships that have involved ridicule and shaming, we can believe in our own ability to change. We can acknowledge the harm done, change our behavior, make amends, and forgive ourselves. Then we will be living in a way that practices respect toward all people, including ourselves.

* For more bibliographic information on *I Deserve Respect* and *Growing Up Again*, see the Bibliography at the end of this article.

HUMOR AS A SOURCE OF HOPE

As I've been writing my thoughts on humor, I keep coming back to the words Phebe Hanson said: ''They're so hungry for humor, you know.'' What is it in humor that we long for? I think what we want from humor is hope. Humor gives us hope that we will be able to express all of our feelings—all the angers, sorrows, fears, joys, affections, serenity, anxieties. We're hungry for closeness to others, for a balanced life. We're hungry for the health that humor can bring and for the tears that bring the deeper healing. Healthy humor is life-affirming. It is a sign of life, and we can follow it to more joyful lives.

HUMOR INVENTORY

You could take some time now to think about humor in your life. You might write down some of your strongest memories and reactions.

- What are some healthy ways you like to enjoy humor?
- How does humor work as a defense mechanism for you?
- Imagine one situation that might be more meaningful to you if you stopped joking around.
- What could you gain if you gave up humor some of the time?
- What kind of pain might you encounter if you stopped joking around?
- What pain has humor helped you avoid?

- When have you used humor to avoid feeling close to someone (to change the subject away from the feeling of intimacy)?
- When you find yourself in a dangerous or stressful situation, what other ways could you relieve stress other than by laughing?
- What are your childhood memories of teasing and ridiculing?
- If you catch yourself being sarcastic or hostile, ask yourself: *What do I feel trapped about? What am I frustrated about? Do I need help in problem solving to get me out of this trap?*
- How can you make amends to others for hurting them with your humor?
- Think of one way you might have a good belly laugh this week.

BIBLIOGRAPHY

Clarke, Jean Illsley, and Connie Dawson. *Growing Up Again: Parenting Ourselves, Parenting Our Children.* Center City, Minn.: Hazelden Educational Materials, 1989.

Potter-Efron, Ronald and Patricia. *I Deserve Respect: Finding and Healing Shame in Personal Relationships.* Center City, Minn.: Hazelden Educational Materials, 1989.

MEN AND CODEPENDENCY

John Hough and Marshall Hardy

As he turned the inside corner of the pub, Mark's eyes met Jim's at the end of the bar. Jim had a drink in his hand, which he waved in a circular manner, the way that signals an invitation to "come on over." As Mark made his way through the crowd, he appreciated that the room was just noisy enough to cover the details of each of the dozen conversations going on.

"How ya doing, buddy!" Jim exclaimed.

"Not bad, Jim, not bad, how 'bout yourself?" replied Mark.

"Better" was Jim's one-word reply. The big smile on his face disappeared as he moved to finish his drink. From the number of straws in front of him it was obvious Jim had left the office early.

Reprinted, with changes, with permission of Hazelden Foundation. Copyright © 1991, by Hazelden Foundation.

Jim was struggling to keep his sanity and some semblance of his marriage alive. This wasn't a good time in his life and hadn't been for over a year.

Mark had gone through a divorce that had culminated two years earlier. Now he was trying to help Jim benefit from his experience and avoid some of the mistakes he had made.

Mark knew from an earlier telephone conversation with Jim that Jim and his wife had left home this otherwise bright, sunshiny morning after another big fight. Maybe she was going to be home this evening and maybe she wasn't.

"Have you called home?" Mark asked. "Do you know if she's there?"

"Naw, not yet," Jim replied.

"So, whose turn is it to pick up little Jimmy?" continued Mark.

"It's her day," said Jim, with a there's-nothing-for-me-to-do-right-now-anyway tone in his voice.

"So, what are you, angry, sad, or drunk?" Mark surprised himself at how straightforward that line came out. Jim responded with a slow turn of his head toward Mark, but said nothing and looked away.

"Look, Jim, one thing I learned was how stupid it is to talk about problems in a bar," Mark said.

"Terrific," replied Jim, "Let's chalk this up to one more thing I can't do right!"

Defining Codependency

Is codependency the same for both men and women? If so, why do so many more women than men report typical codependency symptoms? If not, then what are the key differences between men and women in their experiences of codependency? Are there patterns of codependent thinking, feeling, and behaving that the two genders express in characteristically "masculine" or "feminine" ways?

The most common definition of codependency has been the compulsive need to please, care for, or otherwise help others at the expense of adequately caring for oneself. This sacrifice of one's immediate needs for the sake of others has been assumed to parallel a deeper psychological sacrifice of one's true self as a result of the toxic effects of life within a dysfunctional family.

A problem with this definition is that it addresses the experience of individuals and their families, but not their culture. As a result of this definition by clinicians, women and the very human ability to sacrifice oneself on behalf of others have been unnecessarily pathologized.

Another problem with this definition is that the symptoms of codependency have been so loosely drawn that literally everybody qualifies for the diagnosis. If everyone qualifies for the definition, yet many more women than men are actually "diagnosed," there is obviously something worth questioning about this definition of codependency.

The strength of this definition is how the lives of individuals are understood in the context of their families of origin. The possibility that conditions of an individual's "culture of origin" may also contribute to the development of codependency has only recently been addressed.

Implicit in all understandings of codependency is and

has been the assumption that the problem is a difficulty in the relationship of *two* people, as we saw earlier in Mark's and Jim's marriages. That is the meaning of the prefix *co-* in the term codependency: two and possibly more people become entangled in a web of mutual dependencies. In the original understanding of codependency, one person was an alcoholic while the other was emotionally dependent on the alcoholic and afraid of life on his or her own. As the concept developed, it became apparent that there are numerous possibilities of dependent/dependent and dependent/counter-dependent relationships.

By focusing on what people share in common, instead of an exclusive focus on their individual differences, the codependency concept has the potential to become a "systemic" diagnosis. A more formal yet only preliminary definition of codependency might read as:

> *A pattern of relationship involving two or more individuals who are united by a mutual commitment to care for, protect, or nurture each other's unmet and unrecognized dependency needs.*

This existence of this kind of commitment must be a normal part of all intimate relationships, the difference being only in degree. No one individual can be completely independent all the time. No single relationship is perfectly balanced all the time. All relationships ebb and flow, at times stronger and more conscious, at other times fragile and less conscious. "Am I doing this because I love you as well as need you, or is it just because I need you?'' Who doesn't ask him- or herself that question at some point in a relationship?

Another way of stating this question is to ask, When does the commitment to love, honor, and stay become a facade for a mutually destructive covenant? What are the key indicators that a relationship has stagnated and may be headed toward abuse, addiction, or some other breakdowns? And more specifically, what are the parts that men typically play in this drama?

This chapter is about men, but it is for everyone. That includes women. It's for the man's man: the guy who on the outside seems tough and in charge, yet on the inside is falling apart because his wife has started talking about therapy, apartment hunting, and divorce. It's for the soft male: the polite, apologetic, and even-tempered guy who is so afraid of offending someone that he keeps his personality under wraps.

These issues are shared by men who grew up in intact, healthy families, and those whose family lives were marked by abuse, neglect, or conflict. On the inside many of these men are much the same; that is, they are far more (co-) dependent on others to feel secure and whole than they would ever admit.

Many men don't realize how much more to life there is beyond the specific values our culture has associated with traditional masculinity. These values emphasize an overly responsible attitude toward work, a singular reliance on logical persuasion as a problem-solving strategy, and emotional control as the primary means of regulating self-esteem.

These qualities have clear benefits for the men them-

selves and also their families—under certain circumstances. But, when taken to extremes, the pursuit of
traditional masculine values throws a man off balance.
His life can become empty of all warm, caring feelings;
work and success can become obligations, without any
time out or relief; his relationships can become mun-
dane and listless, or painful and full of conflict. Often
enough, they are doomed to fail.

The relentless pursuit of traditional masculine values
can easily cover a compulsive need to achieve and to
prove one's worth to friends, peers, wives, children,
and, most of all, to oneself. Success at these challenges
lasts only for the moment, then it must be repeated. A
man may appear secure in the face of mounting difficulties in his life. Yet, a closer examination will reveal
that his confidence has been achieved at the expense of
driving his emotional life underground. He has not
achieved confidence so much as he has just become
numb to his fears.

So many men actually fit the stereotype of the thinking-
but-numb-from-the-neck-down automaton. Yet, the
very basis of who men are as individuals, as human
beings, is not what they *think* so much as how they *feel*
about themselves. Without access to his feelings a man
can't help but lose track of who he is, of what his
priorities are, and of what's normal for him. He can
become (or may remain) dependent on others, especially on women, to provide him with the warm fuzzies
of life. Or he does without. He really doesn't have a
relationship with his wife; she has a relationship with
him. The same may be true of his connections with his
children, with his social network, and even with his

own emotional vitality and health. He becomes dependent on some key female in his life to make living worthwhile.

Whether a man's life-style is marked by being tough, domineering, and "independent," or by being soft, reasonable, and pleasing, control is a major factor in his life. He may have first learned to control in order to protect the parts of his personality that to him seemed weak. Maybe he learned that males are supposed to be in control of their wives, their children, and their relationships. Maybe he reached manhood with his concepts of control, independence, and manliness all confused. Maybe his fiancée did as well. Perhaps a few years have passed, and she is beginning to figure it out.

Controlling behavior always ends up by provoking resentments from others, a withdrawal from sharing, and conflict instead of communication. This is how controlling behavior perpetuates the emotional isolation of the controller himself. Others are not going to talk with such a man about what they really believe or how they actually feel about him. Those that can leave, will; those that can't, will compromise.

The consequence of not being involved with the emotional issues of life is that men can become psychologically divorced from all the people they really care about, people whose support is vital and who need these men to be supportive and caring in return. Men often become locked into "masculine" roles that are narrow and hard to manage. These roles make it hard for men to ask for help when it is really needed and deny men the opportunity to talk about important personal issues. These roles severely limit the range of feelings that men can safely express. This restriction of emotional expressiveness is often the chief complaint wives and ex-wives have about the men in their lives.

There is a great mystery about men, among men and women alike. Authentic masculinity remains almost invisible in our culture. This may sound paradoxical since we generally consider our culture to be patriarchal, favoring men over women exactly because of their masculinity. If there is any truth to the saying "It's a man's world," how could there be any mystery about men at all? This chapter examines one part of the mystery of men, an area that has traditionally been off limits in our culture: the emotional self-awareness of men.

A Dysfunctional Family, A Dysfunctional Culture

No man would choose the pain, confusion, exhaustion, and relationship uncertainty characteristic of dysfunctional families if he knew a more healthy and rewarding way to live life. So, how is it he doesn't figure out a better way? What stops him? Part of the problem for men is that there is another source of dysfunctional influence with which they must cope. This is the dominant or parental culture in which men as young boys also receive messages about how to live, love, work, and play. It is termed the *parental culture* because, just like a family, it provides children with a network of values, ideals, customs, roles, expectations, and traditions that shape the ways they think, feel, and behave as adults. The parental culture is to the family of origin what the family is to the individual. It is the family's family.

If the messages from the parental culture are different from the family of origin's dysfunctional rules—if the parental culture's messages are much broader, more tolerant, and more respectful of the boy—then the maturing young man may develop some resistance to the toxic effects of those dysfunctional family rules. There is often hope in the parental culture that has been missing in the parental family, such as a supportive teacher, an understanding coach, or a kind uncle. But there is also danger for the developing boy if the particular message from the parental culture repeats the same message as his dysfunctional family: for example, "real" men are not supposed to show their vulnerable feelings; abused children are supposed to remain loyal to their family and hide their pain.

The parental culture teaches lessons about what is normal for the culture, just as the family of origin does. What is normal for the culture may or may not be normal for a particular family. On the whole, however, the parental culture's lessons express commonly accepted ways to think, feel, and act, or how others should be expected to behave, which everyone in the culture knows about and generally accepts. Examples include: "A good husband is supposed to be a good provider." "Blue is a boy's color; pink is a girl's color." "Do unto others as you would have them do unto you." "When the going gets tough, the tough get going." "Success in life is spelled W-I-N-N-I-N-G." "There is no free lunch." "To complain about pain is unmanly." "Big dogs get all the bones." "Women don't marry shorter men or men who make less money than they do." Different examples, different messages.

Few would agree that this is how things should be, but most recognize that, more often than not, these messages tell the common parable of how things are in the world at large, if not in our little family. Take a minute and play back the tapes of the important messages you received from the parental culture.

Cultural Stereotypes

Another common way of talking about the messages of our parental cultures is to call them stereotypes. Insofar as these messages address all males of one culture, or only the young men, or only young, middle-class Anglo men, they ignore the unique individual differences between men in favor of group characteristics. The parental culture creates stereotypes for its members just like a family creates roles for its members.

Cultural stereotypes are different from family roles in a number of ways. First, and perhaps most importantly, they aren't as easy to identify as roles. Stereotypes get confused with life as it is. Because they are so widespread, because a culture is immeasurably bigger than the largest of families, it is hard for a man to gain the awareness that he is participating in a culturally defined stereotype. Women often try to help men get this distinction. A man's girlfriend slams his apartment door and from the hallway her shout of "MEN!" can be clearly heard. This man may want to examine his behavior for signs of stereotypically "masculine" attitudes.

Family roles have become well identified in the literature of the recovery community. Roles like the family "scapegoat," the "perfect child," the "enabler" are now widely accepted. Family roles involve, at most, only several people. Cultural stereotypes involve all of us. The most basic cultural stereotypes are those having to do with the gender distinctions of masculinity and femininity.

The rules of masculinity define the cultural expectations of the behavior as well as the styles of thinking and feeling characteristic of men. A key rule that defines appropriate male behavior is the one linking masculinity with thinking at the expense of feeling. By following this rule, young men are eager to learn thinking skills and are reluctant to even admit to having a desire for feeling skills. How does this get played out? One very prominent way is in the arena of marriage. A traditional masculine approach to marital conflict emphasizes practical thinking and a focus on concrete events in response to his partner's concern for feelings. The parental culture teaches men to be husbands who ignore their insides and teaches women to be wives who are willing to do the inside work for two. This is a fundamental part of the basic American marriage contract.

Another very prominent male cultural expectation is for men to function as workers and to identify the work they do with who they are. "I am a doctor, lawyer, Indian chief. . . ." The work role becomes equivalent to the self. It seems like boys are trained to be worker bees from birth. They always have to be doing something important or they lose importance as people.

School continues this "education" by rewarding boys for their performance, physical as well as academic. If college is an option, these boys are evaluated further in order to select the "best and the brightest." These young men get the jobs with the highest prestige, salaries, and status. Of course, by definition, as many men "fail" at this competition as succeed. But it doesn't matter what rung of the ladder a man is on; all men know about competition and the pressure to succeed.

Often, when two men meet for the first time, they quickly ask, "Well, what do you do?" And the conversation is likely to continue on work-related topics. This is an example of men making contact with one another, limited to the boundaries of the worker role. It's like a cog in the IBM machine talking with a wheel in the GM machine. We even have the saying, "He's a big wheel in xxx company." No, the job is not who he *is*, it's what he *does*. When a man loses his job he doesn't disappear from the planet. Or does he?

Cultural expectations, like family roles, are often identified by their most prominent behavioral characteristics. These characteristics for male cultural expectations include:

- work as a basis for personal identity
- sex as a means of expressing and receiving intimacy
- vulnerability as weakness and something to be avoided
- competition as a primary means of male-to-male relationship
- achievement and aggression as obligations to perform
- limitations on the degree of feeling easily expressed
- limitations on knowing about relationship issues

- limitations on direct, caring involvement with children

Do you recognize these brief statements as descriptions relevant to your life? Check these ideas out: Does your obligation to work usually or always take precedence over family time? Does your wife complain about your need for sex and at the same time complain how unromantic and closed off to her you seem? Do friends remark that they never can predict when you will open up with them about personal issues? Do you have any really close male friends? Have you noticed within yourself a deep tiredness about how always on the go you are? Do you generally know how you feel? Can you stay in a disagreeable conversation with close friends without getting mad, being abstract, acquiescing, or finding some other exit before there is some closure? Exactly how many minutes of relaxed, caring time did you spend with your children today, yesterday, last week, last year?

If answering these questions is disturbing, you are among the "silent majority" of men. *Silent,* because these issues are seldom discussed among men in a truly constructive manner. They are often discussed in an angry, complaining way by women in the absence of men. *Majority,* because they reflect the cultural conditioning of men, all men, differing only in degree.

So what happens if a man's needs or aspirations lead him to cross the boundary of what's acceptable from the perspective of "normal" male cultural expectations? What if he is one of the many men who discover around the age of forty that there is something missing from his life? Or perhaps he is recovering from an addictive life-style, and he notices that his Twelve Step meeting is completely different from anything else in his life. Maybe he realizes that *he* is completely different in his Twelve Step meeting than he is in his marriage, with his children or friends, or at work.

A grown man faces the same problem as does the child who still lives in a dysfunctional family. If he violates the boundaries of his culture's expectations, he will be on his own. His culture will not support him or even acknowledge his efforts. It may go so far as to punish him for his violation. Hopefully his wife will continue to support him. Hopefully his friends will stay with him. Many men have these kinds of personal relationships, but many don't. Many men have these supportive relationships and don't know it. Or they know but still can't openly allow their wives or friends to be supportive.

The message from the culture is that a man who doesn't work is lazy. And again, there is something obviously wrong with a man who values intimacy over sex, right? Ask any teenage boy and see what kind of response you get. Or ask a teenage girl. They both know the official parental line on questions of sex. They also know what the culture says on the subject as well: Girls are supposed to say no, and boys are *supposed* to say yes.

There are similar expectations about the experience of vulnerability: it is acceptable only under extreme conditions of duress. Or it is acceptable under conditions of manifest, almost guaranteed support and acceptance, like many Twelve Step meetings. Competition, achievement, and aggression are all characteristics that men are supposed to master. If a man shuns competition he invariably feels pressure to explain his reluctance to friends and strangers alike. And what if he doesn't have an explanation? Does that mean he is weak, just weird, or maybe gay?

The expectations that limit the awareness, expression, and participation of men in intimate interactions with their wives are perhaps the most talked about of the "problems" of men. Women write books about this; Oprah Winfrey and other talk-show hosts frequently have public discussions on it. Mental health professionals regularly convene symposia on the subject. Men are constantly on the defensive about this one. It is a complex subject, and it is difficult for many people to talk about.

Great Expectations

These expectations of men gain their power because they define the roles that "real" men are supposed to assume. The roles are not abstractions, they're real life! The greatest challenge to the developing man occurs when he pushes the limits of the roles from his family of origin and his parental culture in the same way and at the same time. Like when he breaks the family denial of his mother's alcoholism, or he asks for help with his dysfunctional marriage by initiating contact with a therapist. Loyal family members and "real men" don't admit to personal problems, nor do they ask for help with them.

The full-speed-ahead, never-surrender model of manhood typified by the John Wayne image in film is giving way to a more flexible, less proud, and more humble model of manhood. It's good that men's ideas about themselves are changing—however slowly. A number of recent studies show that men continue to define themselves and their self-worth in terms of their work and their ability to produce and compete with other men. To beat the other guy still takes precedence over simply being the best a man can be. Men expect it of themselves. Fathers expect it of their sons. Women expect it of men as well, even if they don't like to admit it.

This ethic of always being ready to confront the dragons of the work world is counterproductive as soon as a man crosses the threshold of his home. The reality is, it's not humanly possible for men to check their feelings at the office door and then pick them up again on the way home. No one can turn his feelings on and off like that. The reality is, by the time young men are old enough to work, many have already learned to simply check their feelings . . . period.

One of the most prominent expectations that lives in our culture is the belief that men are supposed to be strong enough, competent enough, and intelligent enough to handle all of their problems, all on their own. Especially personal or emotional problems. This is the expectation that real men are supposed to be "independent." The test of independence is to not need anything or anyone to get by. If a "real man" had to get along on his own, he could. He might even want to.

This is one of the most important of the expectations of masculinity: "real men" are independent of each other and everyone else. The Lone Ranger, the movie image of John Wayne, Hemingway's novel *The Old Man and the Sea* are obvious examples of this expectation that are familiar to many people. There are count-less others. The expectation is about the requirement to prove oneself worthy of respect, worthy of love, and worthy of acceptance. It's also one of the biggest confusions men struggle to sort out in their lives. When the heat is on, men often confuse being independent with being alone, separate, uncommunicative, silent.

Being alone is actually quite easy. The real challenge is to be independent and still be able to share with others. To be independent and also intimate with others. Far too many men end up "independent" and divorced.

One form of this expectation men live up to in public is, Don't wear your feelings on your sleeve. It means men are not supposed to let their deeper feelings show to others. Don't be too emotionally visible to others. It's better to be emotionally opaque than obvious. Of course, after years of practicing deceptions like this, men end up being the ones most confused and out of touch.

The codependent injunctions against talking, trusting, and feeling all have counterparts in the traditional expectations of masculinity. The extreme male stereotype is of a guy who appears *always* sure of himself, *always* tough under pressure, and able to handle *any* problem on his own. He is also typically a guy who *won't talk* about personal issues, is so proud that he *can't trust* anyone to really care for him, and *guards his feelings* against prying eyes.

If you are familiar with the literature on codependency, you will remember that codependents typically end up identifying with those same injunctions. The point is that males grow up with an expectation to minimize their feelings and focus on their thinking. And that is just what most men do: They separate their thinking from their feeling, their heads from their hearts, as a matter of course, codependent or not.

Male Codependency

The concept of codependency began with an implicit assumption that it was about people when, in fact, it was generally about women. That doesn't mean that the term was intended to be a synonym for femininity or with being female. It was not. Yet, as the overlap between codependency and masculinity shows, there is a connection between codependency and the gender expectations of the parental culture.

What follows is our list of characteristics of codependency that are most common in men. Read through the items and listen to your inner reactions. Are we talking about you? Do you recognize the dysfunctional expectations of the parental culture, or the dysfunctional problems of your family of origin?

A codependent man typically

1. buys into a model of masculinity where his psychological, emotional, and spiritual needs are assumed as already met, not wanted, or just not important. He functions on only half of his potential but falsely claims to be fully independent, whole, and happy. As a consequence of all the pretense, he is terrified of being unmasked and will do anything to keep up the facade. Nothing is too expensive, time-consuming, or too much trouble if his pride is at stake.

2. hears from his wife who says that she's taking the kids and leaving, that she's tired and fed up with feeling like she is the only adult in the home. He thinks that he's dedicated his whole life to providing and caring for his family to the very best of his ability, and now it doesn't seem like any of it counts.

3. becomes a provider and protector, especially to partners who are frightened and needy, in an attempt to vicariously fulfill his own needs for psychological closeness, emotional warmth, and spiritual security. He confuses love and providing, and tends to love people who can't provide for or protect themselves. He is in general attracted to weakness and dependence in his love, friendship, and career relationships.

4. has been successful and achieved advancement before others his own age, and then realizes that his kids are afraid of him and his wife is having an affair.

5. is aware of always looking for the approval of older men whom he admires, but it's a secret that he's uncomfortable acknowledging. If he pushes himself he will discover a desire to have received more from his father: his time, his attention, his direct expressions of care and love. He may even realize how important it is to himself to be a better father to his children than his father was to him.

6. may have lost a child and feels overwhelmed with the urge to cry, but can't, then finds himself telling his wife, who is crying, that everything will be okay, there will be opportunity to have another child.

7. finds crises at work to be the only time he experiences real enthusiasm and satisfaction with his job. Otherwise he drones on, on automatic pilot. He is too numb to realize how sick and tired he is of always having to compete with everyone and everything, the constant struggle to stay on guard, the isolation and loneliness of it, and of never being able to just relax without feeling tension.

8. is attracted to emotionally spontaneous and vibrant partners. He may not be sure why women are attracted to him. His partner is the first to discover the limits of their relationship and to become dissatisfied and disappointed. He then finds himself on the defensive. The anticipated separation from this partner feels like a looming catastrophe. When it happens he feels as if he has lost his moorings in life completely.

9. finds sports, hunting, and TV dominate his life outside of work. The power of winning imaginary challenges is more rewarding to him than the "boring" experience of home life. He thinks of himself as having good and close friends, but none of them knows anything at all about how depressed and frightened he is or how long he's been that way.

10. acts as if he is superhuman, always finding the will to rise above others, to be stronger, tougher, more aggressive, more willing to do whatever is necessary to win. Coming home in the evening and having a few drinks is his habitual way of numbing out the feelings of wear and tear from the day. He knows "good liquor" and appreciates a secret feel-

ing of superiority over the mob who just take life as
it is.

11. has a desire to protect his wife from harm or accident, and this desire dominates over other parts of
their relationship. So he sometimes follows her on
the way to work or the store, checks her mail or
phone conversations, and grills her about her activities each time she comes home. It's more than
she wants or appreciates, but he ignores her repeated protests, getting even more suspicious and
resentful as each week goes by.

12. is acutely aware of the "right" expectations in any
situation and is constantly comparing himself
against an internal yardstick of what he should do,
say, think, or feel. He is chronically nervous,
which he passes off through humor. He never really
knows what his options in any situation actually
are and continually settles for far less than his share
of the recognition or respect available to him. On
the other hand, he seldom fails to accept more than
his share of the responsibility, guilt, or blame in an
awkward interaction.

13. is an extremist and believes he must either control
situations, relationships, and partners or be controlled by them. Life is either black or white, right
or wrong, a man's job or a woman's place. He
doesn't have any real friends he trusts, except his
wife, and she is talking about therapy, apartment
hunting, and divorce.

14. may seek mood-altering chemicals, experiences,
or people and can become addicted to the excitement of competition and success. He truly believes

he loves his wife, but has been having one affair after another for years. These behaviors help cover up a tendency toward depression when he is alone with nothing to do. The constant turmoil caused by the addictive behaviors also distracts him from ever focusing in on the shame that is at the center of his life.

15. has lost the ability to distinguish one feeling from another. His body may have become so anesthetized that he isn't sure he has any feelings at all. The only exception is through sex. He can't get enough sex, and his wife can't find enough reasons to avoid it.

16. finds that he is extremely competitive. He is always sizing up situations in order to be at the center of attention, the best, the brightest, the most admirable. It is all so obvious, yet done unconsciously. He doesn't realize that everything in his life is about proving himself to others, and that he has yet to make himself feel proved.

17. feels trapped in a deteriorating relationship he wants desperately to save. What were once his positive attributes—his strength, independence, and stability—are now criticized as his weaknesses, stubbornness, distance, and rigidity. His partner needs him to change in order for her to stay in the relationship. He honestly agrees about the need for that change, but every effort to change feels like he's only doing it to please her. To top it off, she says she doesn't want the changes if he doesn't really mean them. The situation is unbearable. His feelings are threatening to erupt out of control,

maybe ruin everything, so he decides to redouble his efforts to stay on top and control himself. The next thing he hears is their therapist telling him that his rational, logical, and controlling-type thinking is the real problem.

18. may realize that the problem with his not being able to trust anyone with his sad and hurt feelings is that these feelings make him feel small and defenseless, like a child.

19. discovers that his wife is planning a long evening of intimacy that includes as much romance as sex, and he doesn't want to go home because he knows he'll only end up feeling awkward, embarrassed, stupid, and will probably get drunk and angry as a way to end it.

20. avoids acknowledging that he is getting sick until he absolutely can't deny it any longer. Being ill leaves him feeling weak, passive, and incompetent. The pattern is to protest and deny that any problem exists until his partner's concern for his health gets high enough to "force" him to get medical attention.

21. realizes that he has always idealized women. He has read all about the women's movement and equal rights; he has a number of good female friends with whom he can talk, but no male friends at all.

Did you find yourself amid these descriptions? Or a better question might be, How many times did one of them remind you of something? Every man is different. No one can be characterized completely by one definition. Yet estimates range as high as 80 percent of all men in the United States identify strongly with the single description about having wanted more, much more, from their fathers during their growing-up years. What's the significance of this particular feeling? Does that mean you're codependent?

These descriptions highlight some of the problems many men struggle to contain. Men typically hide the reality of these problems from themselves and from each other. Fathers hide these problems from their sons as do sons from their fathers. Women, in part, expect men to keep these problems hidden as well. These problems are so common that the real difference between men is only the degree to which each man's life has been affected.

At heart, these problems stem from the substitution of *stereotypical* male experience in place of *true self* experience. It's about how men have come to believe that a fancy suit called success or toughness or logicalness or emotional control is all that they need to be happy in life. This fancy suit is imaginary. But so many people believe in it, it must be true. . . .

The cultural model of masculinity is only in part a model of codependency. These models overlap because each denies to men the caring, emotional, and vulnerable aspects of being human. This leaves men indirectly and unconsciously dependent on others, wives, secretaries, affairs for their needs for emotional warmth and nurturance.

The truth is that a sexist society subordinates everyone, both men and women. The parental culture teaches little boys to forget their hearts and focus on their heads, and teaches little girls to ignore their heads and develop their hearts. So these little boys are at risk of growing up to be men who have lost touch with their ability to feel, and little girls are at risk of growing up to be women who are uncomfortable with the personal authority to solve their own problems. He is dependent on the freshness of her emotional vitality while she is dependent on his ability to master the world. Together they make a good team, each codependent on the other to create a whole. Add an alcohol abuse problem in him, and the original codependent couple is recreated.

Everyone pays a price for prejudice. Men gain an obvious benefit in terms of political, economic, and social power. But women gain a closer emotional connection to family and friends that is much greater than her mate's. So, who is the winner here? Does it really matter? The challenge for men is to throw off the tough-guy clothes and put on the ordinary garb of everyday life. To do this requires men to learn values about life that are based not on some worn-out script of how things are *supposed* to be, but on the possibilities of what whole, fully human beings *might* be.

Men, Spirituality, and the Way Back to Life

The gradual loss of the natural spiritual dimension in men's lives can be explained, in part, as a consequence of the parental culture's expectations that men are supposed to be separate from their emotions. After all, if you can't tell how you feel from what you think, how can you be sure of the presence of God or a Higher Power in your life? Has anyone ever "thought" his or her way to God? Not likely. Faith is not an intellectual commitment. It is a passionate, whole-life experience.

The spiritual dimension of life is about being able to be passionate about the mysteries of life and the universe. A man's ability to be passionate can extend to having deep feelings about injustice, about his spouse, maybe even about his work. Ultimately, being passionate is about allowing oneself to be carried away into the currents, eddies, and backwaters that make up the stream of life. This "allowing" is another word for "surrendering." This is the difficulty men have with feeling or passion and spirituality: each requires a surrender.

Throughout our history as a country there has been the recognition that in order to maintain a satisfactory balance of life, good emotional, mental, and psychological health, it is necessary to have a firm belief in something wiser, more powerful, and greater than ourselves. Spiritual men and women have been telling us this for all ages. More recently so has the recovery community. Most recently the helping professions have begun to understand and accept spirituality as an integral part of psychotherapy.

The realization is that family, work, feel-good chemicals, food, or dangerous activity must not be allowed to become the most powerful force of life. If some acquisition is all that is needed to feel happy and complete, then the biggest problem of life has been permanently solved. Yet, this solution requires the individual to accept responsibility for making all things work, all the time, all by oneself. Isn't that remarkably similar to the John Wayne image, the "men-are-supposed-to-be-independent" myth? Isn't that part of the general myth about what a "real man" is supposed to be?

Still, for many men the centrality of spirituality in the problem of codependency is difficult to grasp. The overwhelming reality of the human need for spirituality is evident in the fact that every culture throughout history has placed it in the center of its communal life. It is an undeniable human need we have, even if not proven or provable in itself. Yet, our culture appears to be the first to seriously ignore spirituality in favor of disembodied enlightenment, technical advancement, and material comfort.

The recovery community has rediscovered that spirituality is necessary for the further development of all areas of the self. This belief is described in different ways, sometimes as God as we understand Him or Her, or a Higher Power, or simply the great Mystery. Whatever the reference, the importance this community places on spirituality remains consistent.

Spirit Vitalizing Soul

There are a number of ways to draw distinctions and make comparisons between "spirit" and "soul." Are these two different "things" or just two different ways of looking at the same "thing"? How does this question have relevance to the fate of men in their struggles to be more fully human?

An important assumption some make is to identify "soul" as a potential to connect deeply with God and the mystery of all things. This potential for soul resides within every man. It is not in men's heads. It lies dormant deep in their hearts.

Spirituality can be understood as that which activates or energizes soul. When spirituality unites with soul it transforms a potential into a reality. Spirit changes the potential to connect with God to the experience of God's presence. This concept of spirituality emphasizes the meaning of "spirit" as the incorporeal part of man. The part that is not necessarily within the body.

The most important aspect of spirituality is, therefore, where is a man's spirit located? That is, what is the most important focus of a man's life? Where does he place his energies? Where are his values most clearly expressed? If the focus of his "spirit" is external, on his work, his status, his achievements, even his wife, then it is not available to quicken the hollow inside—that is, his soul.

Life in a dysfunctional family works to disempower a boy's spirit. It does so by training him to relate to people and events that are based not on the reality of the circumstances, but on the arbitrary rules that govern what is okay and what is not okay in his family. Consequently, his naturally deep curiosity about life and his potential in it are shamed. His outward-looking self functions to maintain appearances, to keep up with the expectations, rather than to simply be who he naturally is. He feels powerless and trapped. He has a deep and growing emptiness within that yearns to be filled. It desires life!

The metaphor of spirit vitalizing soul carries with it the potential to describe the errant ways in which this union is often sought. Whenever a man resorts to manipulation or control, dishonesty or denial, unquestioned compliance or unrelenting rebellion, drug, alcohol, or other substance abuse, he is in danger of creating a deceptive self. When he finds himself in the grips of those extremist behaviors he risks a further loss of his spirit and with it the potential for his recovery of soul.

The self that emerges from these contortions is accurately termed *deceptive* because it must put on the cloak of normalcy. It must adopt the dysfunctional family's global denial that anything is seriously wrong. There is no abuse going on here! There is nobody but us happy faces in this family! Similarly, our culture values deceptive male behavior: no crying, no complaining, no quitting.

This behavior is deceptive because it is really a performance masquerading as reality. Eventually, it is about a man who has never been able to truly know himself as an individual separate from his behavior. It is about a man who has so confused who he is with what he does that he cannot tell the difference. In fact, there is no difference in his experience. Deprive him of his role and he feels the pain of abandonment down to his core. He must maintain the deception that he is happy, secure, confident, optimistic, and so much more. His family and his culture both whisper in his ear, "Don't you do anything different, everything will be okay, just tough it out a little longer." Only it never ends.

Understanding the Loss

A common way a man gets in touch with the futility of this strategy is to lose his spouse or family or both. Deprived of his wife and her supplies of nurturance, he feels abandoned. He feels cut loose from his moorings. Empty. Soulless. He is unable to care for himself. He has always been symbiotically tied to external sources of support, and now he is cut off. His work or other friends no longer have the same meaning. A profound sadness overwhelms him. Spirit is not at home within this man's soul.

Not only do these men feel the loss of the relationship, but if they stay with their feelings long enough they will discover that they feel lost as well. On their own they feel incomplete, incompetent, and not confident. It is at this point that they begin to understand how dependent on external support they have been.

A frequent comment men make at this point is about how tired they feel. How really deeply bone-tired they are. They realize how much energy has been invested in keeping up the status quo, controlling so much, denying so much. They also get the picture of how much they have missed out on because they've been "too busy." And with that realization comes the knowledge that they cannot make themselves happy, they cannot take care of themselves.

Men in this stage of crisis realize they have really been out in left field about what is truly important in life. They can't keep up the pretense any longer. They are face-to-face with the knowledge that their deepest suffering is from the pain of the inner spiritual well gone dry. They find themselves alone within walls they have built themselves.

Accepting Desperation

If necessity is the mother of invention, then desperation is the introduction to necessity: "I am a man, just a normal human being, and I can't make it on my own. I need help!'' What a statement for a man to make. All the rules and expectations about what "real men" are supposed to do, say, think, and feel are broken in one fell swoop.

But, how much desperation does it take for a "real man" to admit that he has limitations? The problem with men is they don't know when to quit. The indoctrination into the value system that rewards only the victor and immediately forgets the second-place fella is powerful. "When the going gets tough, the tough get going." Yes, that is often true. But is it always true, in every circumstance, on every occasion? Is competition the only way to live? Does everything of value have to be earned?

How is it even possible to "earn" one's worth? Isn't that just a little pretentious? Yet, the parts of men that play at being God believe in the absolute necessity of earning one's way, for everything.

Many men in Twelve Step recovery programs have found that nothing can nurture the soul but the return of the spirit. No amount of achievement will ever "earn" enough spirit. It is a gift, the spirit, no charge. But, how is it found? Where do you go to get spirit? For most men, the answer is found in the desperation that accompanies personal crisis. The only logical thing to do with genuine desperation is to surrender, to quit, to acknowledge powerlessness and *put down the burden*! Many first learn of this concept in the acknowledgment of powerlessness found in Step One of their Twelve Step program. The immediate result of surrender is the opening of the heart to compassion.

Practicing Compassion

Where desperation marks a man's entry into crisis, compassion indicates the way out. Compassion is a form of love. It is the possibility that "I," here on the inside, is like "you," there on the outside.

Most men who are in the stage before crisis, the point where they are still hopeful of "beating this thing," know inside that they are not doing so well. They struggle with the feelings of being not equal to or one-down to others with whom they come in contact. They struggle with poor self-esteem, a lack of self-confidence, and constant tension. Their need is to feel more equal. What gets in their way is the pretense they have put up that they do feel equal, the "everything-is-just-fine-I'm-doing-great-how-'bout-you?" attitude. What a burden!

Surrender releases men from having to pretend to others that they are okay when they are not okay. The feeling of compassion indicates accepting someone just as he or she is. There is no judgment of the person's qualifications. It is the ultimate free gift. Receiving compassion is the experience of being valued without having to first earn or achieve anything. The experience of compassion says, "I'm okay just the way I am." It means the burden of pretense can be left behind. What a relief! For a man in crisis, this is a godsend.

With compassion securely anchored inside comes the possibility of developing an inner peacefulness and the ability to relax and enjoy life's small pleasures. This "peace that passes understanding" provides a safe inner haven inside against the tumult and inconsistency of the outer world's expectations and demands. The spirit has returned to the soul. A man now has an inner place that always feels full, even as the outer world withholds nurturance and continues to make conflicting demands.

The pathways to recovery and health begin as a crisis that many men resist. As the pridefulness of the I-can-handle-my-problems-myself attitude wears thin, a new possibility emerges—that of surrender. The result is a vulnerable time where the possibilities for connections between us and the Mystery of the living web outside to which we belong are at their greatest. It is a seemingly paradoxical relationship. To get outside and back into life, a man must first quit life and go inside. That is where spirit and soul reside.

In closing, let's return to Jim and Mark, the men we met at the beginning of this chapter.

Jim's head popped around Mark's office door; seeing no one was there but Mark, he came in and sat down. "Guess what?" he said.

"I don't know," replied Mark, "but from the look of it, it's pretty good."

"Yeah," said Jim, "it is. Anne and I are moving back in together this weekend," he said. While his eyes dropped a little, the smile on his face stayed put.

"That's great," beamed Mark, "that's terrific."

"Yeah, I'm really happy about it; so is Anne," Jim confessed. It was still awkward for Jim to talk about himself, but he could do it with Mark. "I didn't think this would ever happen," Jim continued after a pause. "I know I've got a lot more to learn—we have to learn," he said, correcting himself, "but at least we're doing it together. I can't tell you how much I

breathe easier these days, Mark, how much less I worry about things.''

"Hey, buddy, I am glad for you,'' Mark replied. "I know how important this has been for you.''

"Yeah, I used to think the problems in my life were never going to change,'' Jim said with a laugh. "Now I feel like I've got a new lease on life, another chance, and I'm going to make it work.''

THE TWELVE STEPS
OF ALCOHOLICS ANONYMOUS*

1. We admitted we were powerless over alcohol—that our lives had become unmanageable.
2. Came to believe that a Power greater than ourselves could restore us to sanity.
3. Made a decision to turn our will and our lives over to the care of God *as we understood Him.*
4. Made a searching and fearless moral inventory of ourselves.
5. Admitted to God, to ourselves, and to another human being the exact nature of our wrongs.
6. Were entirely ready to have God remove all these defects of character.
7. Humbly asked Him to remove our shortcomings.
8. Made a list of all persons we had harmed, and became willing to make amends to them all.
9. Made direct amends to such people wherever possible, except when to do so would injure them or others.
10. Continued to take personal inventory and when we were wrong promptly admitted it.
11. Sought through prayer and meditation to improve our conscious contact with God *as we understood Him,* praying only for knowledge of His will for us and the power to carry that out.
12. Having had a spiritual awakening as the result of these steps, we tried to carry this message to alcoholics, and to practice these principles in all our affairs.

*The Twelve Steps of A.A. are taken from *Alcoholics Anonymous*, 3rd ed., published by A.A. World Services, Inc., New York, N.Y., 59-60. Reprinted with permission. Alcoholics Anonymous is for recovery from alcoholism, and Twelve Step programs patterned after A.A. address other problems.

THE TWELVE STEPS
OF AL-ANON*

1. We admitted we were powerless over alcohol—that our lives had become unmanageable.
2. Came to believe that a Power greater than ourselves could restore us to sanity.
3. Made a decision to turn our will and our lives over to the care of God *as we understood Him.*
4. Made a searching and fearless moral inventory of ourselves.
5. Admitted to God, to ourselves, and to another human being the exact nature of our wrongs.
6. Were entirely ready to have God remove all these defects of character.
7. Humbly asked Him to remove our shortcomings.
8. Made a list of all persons we had harmed, and became willing to make amends to them all.
9. Made direct amends to such people wherever possible, except when to do so would injure them or others.
10. Continued to take personal inventory and when we were wrong promptly admitted it.
11. Sought through prayer and meditation to improve our conscious contact with God *as we understood Him*, praying only for knowledge of His will for us and the power to carry that out.
12. Having had a spiritual awakening as the result of these steps, we tried to carry this message to others, and to practice these principles in all our affairs.

ABOUT THE AUTHORS

Stephanie Abbott is the author of *Forgiveness: The Power and the Process*, and the very popular Hazelden pamphlet, *Codependency: A Second Hand Life*. She is president of the National Foundation for Alcoholism Communications in Seattle. She writes a column called "Family Matters" in the professional magazine *The Counselor*.

Melody Beattie is the author of three nationally bestselling books: *Codependent No More*, *Beyond Codependency: And Getting Better All the Time*, and *The Language of Letting Go*. Her inspirational writing has motivated thousands of people to find healthier, more peaceful lives.

Brian DesRoches works in Seattle where he has a private counseling practice, focusing on issues surrounding codependency and chemical dependency. DesRoches is the author of *Working Through Conflict* and *Faces of Recovery*, published by Hazelden Educational Materials, and *Reclaiming Your Self: The Codependent's Recovery Plan*, published by Dell.

Marshall Hardy, Ph.D., CADAC, is the coauthor of *Against the Wall: Men's Reality in a Codependent Culture*. He has extensive experience working with adult male children of dysfunctional families, male codependents, and men with post-traumatic stress. A certified alcoholism and drug abuse counselor with a doctorate in counseling psychology, he has been nationally recognized for his consultation and training contributions to treatment and employee assistance programs. He pioneered the first Male CoDA (Codependents Anonymous) meetings and T.R.A.C. men's groups (for men in Transition, Recovery Adjustment, and Codependency). Currently he is president of Hardy and Associates and executive director of a men's resource center.

John Hough, Ph.D., is the coauthor of *Against the Wall: Men's Reality in a Codependent Culture*. He is a psychotherapist in Houston, Texas, where he specializes in the treatment of men and in male psychology. He holds a doctorate in psychology and trained extensively in VA Hospitals, where his interest in men's issues developed. He has developed a gender-sensitive model of inpatient treatment for men with codependency. He continues to write on the subject of male psychology and psychotherapy. He is a member of the Men's Health Network, a private practice association that specializes in therapy and educational services for men and their families.

Roseann Lloyd, who received an M.A. from the University of Minnesota, is coauthor of *True Selves: Twelve Step Recovery from Codependency,* and *JourneyNotes: Writing for Recovery and Spiritual Growth,* both published by Hazelden Educational Materials. She is the cotranslator of *The House with the Blind Windows,* the story of a girl coming of age in an alcoholic family, and she is one of the authors of Hazelden's *Today's Gift: Daily Meditations for Families.* Having studied poetry at the University of Montana with Tess Gallagher and Richard Hugo, Ms. Lloyd's poems appear in many literary journals and in *Minnesota Writes: Poetry,* an anthology published by Milkweed Editions. A recent recipient of a Loft-McKnight grant for her work, Lloyd lives in Minneapolis and teaches writing. She also works as a writing consultant for groups and individuals.

Veronica Ray is a free-lance writer. She is the author of *Choosing Happiness: The Art of Living Unconditionally,* and *Design for Growth: Twelve Steps for Adult Children,* both published by Hazelden Educational Materials. She also wrote the *Moment to Reflect* meditation series for Hazelden.

Brenda Schaeffer is author of *Loving Me, Loving You: Balancing Love and Power in a Codependent World, Is It Love or Is It Addiction?* and the four pamphlets in Hazelden's Healthy Relationship Series. A licensed psychologist and a certified transactional analyst, she lectures nationally and internationally. She is an experienced psychotherapist, trainer of therapists, lecturer, and communications consultant. She has trained with experts in hypnosis, Gestalt, bioenergetics, visual imagery, existential, transpersonal, regression, and developmental psychologies. A Clinical and Provisional Teaching Member of International Transactional Analysis Association, she is Director of Brenda M. Schaeffer and Associates in Minneapolis, where she conducts training, workshops, and therapy.

Jennifer P. Schneider, M.D., Ph.D., is a physician specializing in internal medicine and addiction medicine. She is the author of *Back from Betrayal: Recovering from His Affairs* and the coauthor of *Sex, Lies, and Forgiveness: Couples Speaking Out on Healing from Sex Addiction* and *Rebuilding Trust: For Couples Committed to Recovery*, both published by Hazelden Educational Materials. She lectures widely on sex addiction, coaddiction, and codependency.

"EASY DOES IT BUT DO IT"
with Hazelden Recovery Books

THE 12 STEPS TO HAPPINESS *by Joe Klaas*
36787-1 $4.95

BARRIERS TO INTIMACY: For People Torn by Addictive and Compulsive Behavior *by Gayle Rosellini and Mark Worden*
36735-9 $4.95

BACK FROM BETRAYAL: A Ground-Breaking Guide To Recovery For Women Involved With Sex Addicted Men *by Jennifer Schneider, M.D.*
36786-3 $4.95

LIVING RECOVERY: Inspirational Moments for 12 Step Living *by Men and Women in Anonymous Programs*
36785-5 $4.95

COMPULSIVE EATERS AND RELATIONSHIPS *by Aphrodite Matsakis, Ph.D.*
36831-2 $4.95

CREATING CHOICES: How Adult Children Can Turn Today's Dreams into Tomorrow's Reality *by Sheila Bayle-Lissick and Elise Marquam Jahns*
37378-2 $4.99

SHOWING UP FOR LIFE: A Recovering Overeater's Triumph Over Compulsion *by Heidi Waldrop*
37379-0 $4.99

These bestsellers are available in your local bookstore, or order by calling, toll-free 1-800-733-3000 to use your major credit card.

Prices and order numbers subject to change without notice. Valid in U.S. only.

For information about the Hazelden Foundation and its treatment and professional services call 1-800-328-9000. In Minnesota call 1-800-257-0070. Outside U.S. call (612) 257-4010.